GW00647443

Legends of

THE GLASGOW &
SOUTH WESTERN RAILWAY

in LMS days

DAVID L. SMITH

DAVID & CHARLES
Newton Abbot London North Pomfret (Vt)

British Library Cataloguing in Publication Data

Smith, David Larmer
    Legends of the Glasgow & South Western Railway in
    LMS days.
    1. Glasgow and South Western Railway – History
    I. Title
    385'.09414   HE3040.G/

    ISBN 0–7153–7981–X

Library of Congress Catalog Card Number: 80–66093

© David L. Smith 1980

Typeset by Northern Phototypesetting Co, Bolton
and printed in Great Britain
by Biddles Limited, Guildford, Surrey
for David & Charles (Publishers) Limited
Brunel House Newton Abbot Devon

Published in the United States of America
by David & Charles Inc
North Pomfret Vermont 05053 USA

Contents

CONTENTS

1

The Reformers

In the early hours of 1st January 1923 I wrote in my diary '. . . and so 1922 went out peacefully under a full moon. So also went out the old Sou'West.'

I wrote that sentimentally, but perhaps dutifully, as one who had loved the old Glasgow & South Western Railway, but I cannot recall any feeling of acute regret. The real Sou'West, the Sou'West that *we* knew, had gone years before. James Manson, locomotive superintendent, had retired in 1912. Since then we had had one successor who swept all G&SW engines aside as unworthy, and another who meddled incompetently with these engines until hardly a one was working at former full strength. I know that they *looked* well – never had G&SW engines been so artistically painted, but paint does not help you to keep time on the Pullman, or to climb Glendoune bank. Yes, those final years of the G&SW had not been happy ones. Sick at heart with the Whitelegg regime, I turned with a high hope to this great new idea, this 'Grouping', which promised us light in our darkness.

I was still far from the centre of things, but I had read avidly of the new set-up, of our new companions with whom we had to go forward shoulder-to-shoulder. We were to be in the 'group' called the London, Midland & Scottish Railway. We were to be 'grouped' with the Caledonian Railway, the Highland, the London & North Western, the Midland, and some smaller English railways. There were great prospects here. Surely in the organisations of those great companies there were those with the perception to comprehend and arrest this destruction of our fine engines.

Curiously enough, it was of the L&NW that I thought in our

5

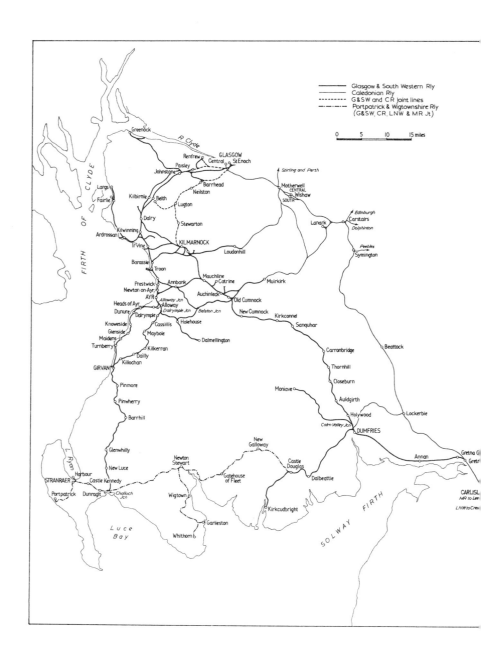

extremity. The L&NW – hardly a railway publication could you open without finding accounts of the prowess of their engines – George the Fifths, Prince of Wales, Claughtons. And they had *hundreds* of them! Surely they could spare us a few to run our trains more efficiently. I pictured a Claughton on the Pullman, a George the Fifth on the 5.10pm Glasgow to Ayr, a Prince of Wales on the Stranraer Road. A wilder flight of fancy glimpsed a Claughton tearing down from Dalnaspidal with a 2–4–0 Jumbo as pilot. I did not know, or had forgotten, that such locomotives would require a somewhat severe haircut and shave before they could have gone under some of our Scottish bridges.

It began to dawn upon me that our first foreign contacts were to be not with those big English railways, but with the Scottish Caledonian. The Caledonian – that marvellous railway with the blue engines and the black-and-white coaches – the Caley, of the Dunalastairs and *Cardean*. Oh, I knew the traditional hatred of the G&SW men for the Caley. That was none of my business. The Caley had a name for efficiency in locomotive matters. Surely their advent would be for good.

As might have been expected, one of the earliest changes came at Muirkirk, where the G&SW made end-on junction with the Caley. There the warring nations appeared to work amicably together, and Charlie Wilson, with his Caley 4–4–0 No 1083 were honoured guests in the G&SW shed. In February 1923 Charlie's fireman was sent with G&SW driver Tom Floyd to work on the Muirkirk-Ayr trains, while Floyd's fireman went with Charlie on the Carstairs jobs.

Rather strangely, one of the first new moves affected our three Dalmellington passenger guards, James Brechany, James McCulloch, and Adam Dick. On the late shift they ran the 12.45pm to Ayr and the 2.30pm to Muirkirk. There they rested till a Caley crew took a connecting train to Carstairs and back, after which they ran the 7.00pm to Ayr. It was an obvious economy for the Ayr train and men to go right through to Carstairs and back, so they were put to learning the road. When Adam Dick got to Sandilands the first trip they gave him a big pair of nippers and told him to check tickets. 'And,' said Adam, 'the first thing I did was I chackit ma thoomb!'

Adam got a bit of a fright one night on this job. It was old Westinghouse stock and coming up Poniel bank they began to drag a bit. Old Charlie Wilson looked back and saw sparks. 'Jock,' he said, 'I think there's a brake stickin' on that third cairriage.' 'Right,' said the fireman. He dropped off, caught the third coach, sat on the lower footboard and pulled the release wire. Then he dropped off again and caught the van. So Adam Dick was sitting quietly in his seat when in the middle of the section the door banged open and a big lanky figure bounced in, shut the door, plumped down in the opposite seat and lit a cigarette! Apparently this was a not-unusual performance.

Incidentally, the guards told me that the permanent way between Muirkirk and Lanark was in a shocking condition. One of them said you could get a smoother run in a coal cairt.

Then came the innovation of the Perth goods. There was nothing very wonderful about this. For years this train had run from Perth to Glasgow (General Terminus). This was merely a 40-mile extension of its run to Ayr, but to the Ayr men, Perth seemed as far away as Northern Norway. To understand their attitude, you must think of the quality of coal supplied to Ayr shed in March 1923. You got a mineral train from Ayr harbour to Waterside, 13.9 miles. At Waterside you took the long shovel and dug about half-a-ton of dirt and clinker out of your fire. Bargany coal was the worst – it was mainly stone, with little heat in what coal there was, and Houldsworth was about as bad. To come from *Perth* – it was inconceivable. On 12 March in came the engine of the Perth goods, Caley 0–6–0 No 653. At Ayr shed all were watching . . . The Caley fireman had no long shovel on his engine! He put the poker through his fire, threw the poker on the tender, and went to his lodgings! For the return trip they gave him five hutches of Bargany and two of Houldsworth. He had to clean his fire at West Street and again at Larbert!

No 878 came in the next morning. During the day there came an urgent message from Perth. 'See that the 3.10 engine is

supplied with the best coal you have.' They gave him their best –
seven hutches of Bargany! The Ayr men chortled. This would
show them. Now there would be an improvement. There was.
Down came a wagon of lovely coal – Muirkirk splint, labelled 'To
be reserved for the engine of the Perth goods' . . .

The Caley influence was spreading. Down with the Muirkirk-
Ayr train came Muirkirk's Caley guard Peter Mackie, with his
silver braid, cheese-cutter cap, patent-leather belts and pouch,
looking a bit like the commissionaire of a West End theatre.
Charlie Wilson began to work down also, with No 1083. Charlie
had little decoration about him, a little wizened unimpressive
figure, but he was a master engineman. Then after a time the
Muirkirk men got No 1060, one of the Drummonds which had
been rebuilt with the Dunalastair I boiler. A marvellous engine it
was – Muirkirk's G&SW men said that they never had the like of
her. Tom Morton drove No 1060 for a long while. They say that
Carstairs was furious at losing her.

There was no mistaking the Caley influence when it came to
train loads. The G&SW had always treated its engines tenderly.
Maximum loads were set well within engine capacity. However,
the new rulers believed in making an engine work for its living.

They bent an eagle eye on the Ayr harbour-Waterside jobs.
These, since the ironworks closed down in 1921, were plain and
straight – empties up, coal down. The distance is 13.9 miles; 10
miles from Ayr to Patna are heavy pulling, with a ruling grade of 1
in 70. The most powerful engines then on the job were the
Drummond 0–6–2 tanks, with $18\frac{1}{4}$in cylinders and 180lb/sq in
boiler pressure. G&SW load tables allowed those engines a
maximum of 33 empties on the uphill journey. 'Ridiculous,' said
the planners, 'an engine of those dimensions should take up 45
empties at least.' So on 24 September 1923 they loaded up the
11.40am from Ayr harbour with 45 empties and a 20-ton Caley
brake van. They were given 0–6–2T No 10, one of the 1919 batch
which had the larger tanks with 1910 gallons capacity. Jimmy
McLean of Ayr was driving, and there were two locomotive
department inspectors aboard.

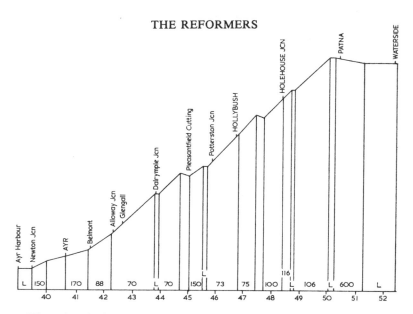

They battled up to Dalrymple Junction, $4\frac{3}{4}$ miles, and there they had to stop to fill the boiler, the water being almost out of sight in the glass. Then they went on to Potterston Junction, another two miles, and there they found that No 10's tanks were nearly dry. As there was no column before Waterside, nearly six miles away, they could only put their train into the Coylton road and run light down to Ayr for water. Back up, they got going again, but had to stop at Holehouse to fill the boiler. They got to Waterside eventually, cleaned the fire, and got 45 wagons of coal for the return journey. They stopped at Patna and pinned down 18 brakes. This was overdoing it, and on the short rise into Pleasantfield cutting before Dalrymple Junction they *stuck*. They released some brakes, re-started and broke a wagon drawhook. So they had to take one part of the train down to Dalrymple Junction, put it in the down line siding, and come back for the other lot. Quite a day.

That settled them for a while. It was 4 March 1924 before they tried again, this time with No 11 (ex-122), one of the original Drummond 0–6–2Ts of 1916, 45 wagons on, driver Andy Rennie and two inspectors. Even with only the 1800-gallon tank they got up without mishap, but took 64 minutes instead of the scheduled 52. Coming down, they had 38 wagons of coal and got down all right, but could not have stopped at Alloway Junction had it been necessary. This, however, was considered satisfactory; 45 empties were to be the regular load. Two days later, both the 11.40am and a later special ran short of water. Tam Young shoved his train in at Potterston and returned to Ayr for water. He got into a traffic jam at Ayr and did not get back for an hour and a half.

On 17 March a Caley 0–8–0 tender engine arrived at Ayr. This was LMS No 17990, ex-CR No 600, the pioneer Caley 0–8–0, with Westinghouse brake and lever reverse. On 19 March she made a trip to Waterside with brake van only. On 21 March she ran the 11.40am, taking 51 empties and van, and kept time, Dan Johnstone driving. They took 43 wagons of coal coming down. Dalrymple Junction noted that she was 'going very fast'.

On 24 March 1924 I noted: 'The 0–8–0 again on 11.40. Brought up 50 and in afternoon brought up 24. Blowing very badly from dome joint and smokebox door burned. R. McMurtrie driving.' Again: '29/3/24. 17990 is working away, but not doing very well. She has heating boxes, steams poorly and is sore on coal. They have to hand the door, and one day they had a Caley inspector aboard. He was taking a spell at the firing when the door fell in, handle and all.' '4/4/24. 17990 going on, but apparently rather hard pressed at the job, for both injectors require to be on the whole road, and as a result, her firebox stays have been leaking badly. I am informed that she consumes something like thirteen hutches ($6\frac{1}{2}$ tons) of coal for the double journey to Waterside (56 miles), and takes about 3500 gallons of water for one uphill journey. Houston Paterson on her this week.' I may say that Houston Paterson got the name of being the one man who could get any reasonable results from the 0–8–0, but even then she was pretty awful. The Potterston signalman told me that from passing Alloway Junction to passing Holehouse Junction, the regular time of the 0–8–0 was one hour. The distance is exactly six miles . . .

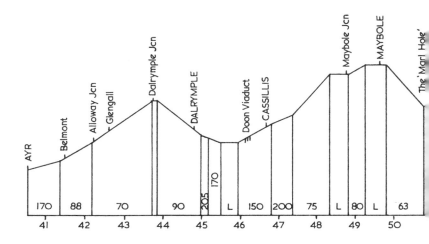

In the middle of May 1924 another eight-coupler was sent to Ayr, No 17994. It was said to be a little better than 17990; in September she was taken away, and Ayr got Peter Drummond's pioneer 0–6–0 No 71 (ex-279) for the Waterside road, the first of 'the Pumpers'! There was not much 'Pumper' about them by that time. The pumps had gone in favour of injectors, the steam driers had gone; so had the feedwater heaters. the Pumpers settled down on the Waterside road, and I must say gave a deal less trouble than the eight-couplers. Of course you had to shovel coal and keep on shovelling, and you did not need to be in a hurry. I saw Andy Bryan, with 71 and 50 empties, take 30 minutes for the $3\frac{1}{4}$ miles passing Ayr station to passing Dalrymple Junction. Ayr got five Pumpers eventually.

After that the reformers sought fresh fields for their efforts; they took up the case of the night goods from Glasgow to Stranraer. For many years this had run as a through train, Glasgow men working to Stranraer the one night and back the next, Stranraer men taking the opposite turn. Over the years there had come changes, and by the time of the Grouping it had become a sort of relay race, with Glasgow men working to Ayr, Ayr men to Girvan and Girvan men to Stranraer. The return working was hardly recognisable as a through train. Engines employed were

12

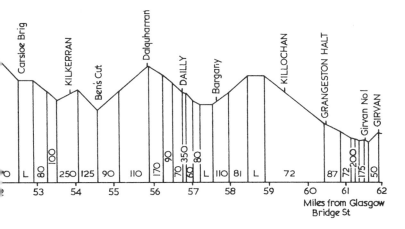

Miles from Glasgow
Bridge St

little G&SW 0–6–0s with 18in cylinders and 150lb/sq in boiler pressure. A pilot was taken usually from Ayr to New Luce. Loads were moderate, about 40 wagons Ayr to Girvan and 28 south of that. There were reasons for this restraint. Look at the gradient profile, Ayr to Girvan. Did you ever see anything more calculated to break couplings on a non-fitted train? The G&SW men knew that with two engines going pell mell down the banks and the guard holding tight in the rear, they could *just* manage to keep the couplings tight through the dips on 40 wagons, not more. South of Girvan, on those even heavier gradients a van might in the case of a breakaway hold 28 wagons, but not more.

The scorn of the reformers knew no bounds – two engines, for 28 wagons! Forget it! Bring bigger engines, legislate for bigger loads! Right at the start they encountered a snag. This service had to use $7\frac{1}{4}$ miles of the Portpatrick & Wigtownshire section to reach Stranraer, and at the moment the PP&W was banned to heavy engines pending extensive relaying. They had to start with one of Manson's 17 class 0–6–0s – no great increase in power. The new train left College goods station in Glasgow at 1.00am, arriving Stranraer about 7.00am. The enginemen, from Corkerhill shed, then booked off in Stranraer, leaving that evening with the 6.35pm goods, due at College about midnight. The new

13

1.00am at once loaded up heavily, and Ayr had to provide a pilot through to New Luce practically every morning.

It was not an ideal arrangement, for hardly any of the Corkerhill men of that period had ever worked goods trains south of Ayr. They had to be conducted by men who were not very sure themselves, and had not handled such big loads. By the summer of 1924, the reformers had bullied the engineer's department into permitting the use of a Drummond 0–6–0 on this job. Corkerhill had four of the Pumpers, Nos 82–5 (ex 302–5). After that the reformers really went to town. Even the Pumpers could not take unaided the loads which were now offering. All right, give them a pilot from Ayr, but give them *both* something to do. New top limits were set: between Ayr and Girvan, 'equal to 80' of goods, south of Girvan, 'equal to 50'.

Well, here was a proposition! 80 between Ayr and Girvan! You just couldn't do it. Look, for instance at just one snag. Come down the bank from milepost 51¾ to Kilkerran. At the bridge leading to Carsloe farm there is a little bit of level. Pull as you like, there are a number of wagons in the middle of the train which will slow up on that level. The weight of the wagons behind them slackens their couplings, then they tip over the edge of the 1 in 80; bang go all the slack couplings and it's an even chance that something breaks. However, orders were orders. As soon as they were over Maybole the drivers started piling it on until they were going down the banks like twin volcanoes. In the rear the guard had his brake screwed on to the last ounce of his energy. If they were lucky, they got a big train through with only some furious 'rugs' at the bad bits; if they were not, it broke away. If that happened, they kept on for Girvan as fast as the wheels would go round, lest the rear portion come down on top of them. After that they would go back on the down road and look for the rear half, quite difficult on a dark morning with only Kilkerran box open.

Kilkerran got the full benefit. The station sits on a patch of moss, and with any train at all you feel the vibration. A new station-master came to Kilkerran. He and his wife were in bed when about 4.00am came the 1.00am – two engines, maybe 70

14

wagons, maybe at 65mph! The stationmaster's wife got out of bed and ran for her life. There was a Kilkerran signalman who used to go out and stand in the middle of the road when the 1.00am went by. He was quite convinced that one morning the box would come tumbling down about his ears.

How the Pumpers stood it I do not know. They must have got the cottered big ends by that time. Also the vans. Jock Geddes had a Midland inspector with him in the van one morning. Jock got his length of point-rodding on to the end of the brake handle, and he had it screwed up till the fire was flying in sheets as they came down on Kilkerran. The Midland man was about off his head. 'The van'll never stand it! It'll never stand it!' he cried. He went out and sat on the floor of the end platform with his feet on the step outside ready to jump when it disintegrated. They had a standard LMS four-wheeled 20-ton van on it at that time. It was reaching Stranraer of a morning with four slack tyres. They thought that to spread the load, they would try a Caley six-wheeled 20-ton van. The only difference was that when it got to Stranraer there were *six* slack tyres!

It *was* pretty hard on stock, and Carlisle sent Corkerhill four more Pumpers to help out. They also sent No 61 (ex 121), one of the Drummond 2–6–0 superheaters, which Jimmy Walker got. No 61 still had the Hasler speed recorder, and they were getting 70mph on the dial at times going through Kilkerran. This locomotive was so easy on coal and water that the men on the Pumpers must have envied her crew. Sanny Mann and Ronald Canovan had No 83 on the 1.00am one morning. There was obviously something seriously wrong – they shovelled in *seven* tons of coal between Glasgow and Stranraer. A valve casing had split and was blowing in the smokebox.

I am sorry that I never managed to get a run on the 1.00am in the wild old days. I was a bit under the weather then. But in after years I made the acquaintance of the men who had run the job, and their tales of their experiences were great compensation. Jimmy McGee, Jimmy Walker, Jimmy Sewell, Bob Raeburn, Bob Caldow, Harry Barr, Archie Davie – those were some of the men who ran this job, surely one of the most sensational footplate experiences in the British Isles.

Passenger train loads were piling up too. The LMS had restored the 'Daylight Service' (Larne-Stranraer and back, summer only). The connecting trains, 12.25pm from Stranraer harbour and 3.55pm from Glasgow, were quite hard booked south of Ayr, and in 1925 42-ton LNW dining cars were added. Girvan men worked to Stranraer with the 5.20am ex-Glasgow and returned with this 12.25pm 'Midday Paddy'. By 1925 the PP&W track was a bit more stable, so a superheated Drummond 4-4-0 was sent to Girvan for this turn – Corkerhill's No 325 (ex-137), the one with the right-hand drive. Girvan did not have much luck with her. Superheater tubes gave constant trouble. No 330 (ex-152) was sent from Carlisle as replacement but was in very poor condition itself. For the summer of 1926 Girvan got another from Carlisle, No 14518 (ex-327, ex-139), which did quite well. In 1927 No 330 came back, repaired and renumbered 14521; a splendid engine, and they had a great summer with her.

In summer, Ayr men took on the 3.55pm instead of the 4.10pm. They were told to put a Drummond engine on the job. Ayr had six of the older, non-superheated batch. One, No 331 (ex-131) had been rebuilt with superheater, but it was too busy on the Glasgow road standing in for heating Baltics. They tried the non-superheaters on the Stranraer job a few times, but they were as bad as ever – slow as a funeral on the uphill, and treacherous on the downhill with sudden wild rolling. So they just went back to their Manson 18 class engines, which were not brilliant.

By 1927, two years of hard work had worn the Mansons still more. Piloting was frequent. No 14518 arrived at Ayr, with a message from R. Killin that she was to be put on this 3.55pm job. On 19 June 1927 up came No 14518, with driver Archibald Ross, universally known as 'Poker'. He had never had a Drummond on the Stranraer road before, and he went rioting down the banks as he was wont to do with a Manson. That run was a classic. I gathered that the crew had quite a job to stay on. Big lumps of coal were bouncing off the tender and smashing on the faceplate.

Above: LMS No 16423, P. Drummond 0-6-2T ex G&SW 84/24.
D. L. Smith collection

Below: LMS No 17756, P. Drummond 0-6-0 ex G&SW 297/77.
J. J. Cunningham

Above: Kilkerran station, looking south.
E. M. Patterson

Below: LMS No 14521, P. Drummond, 4-4-0 ex G&SW 152/330.
K. Nichols

However, they got back alive and Poker began to fancy himself as a runner. There were some rough passages. I never sampled any of them, but I got a lot of quiet amusement from the touchline. When Poker got the right-away at Ayr he used to yank open the regulator and shout 'Here we go! Hell or Belfast!' Then complaints began to come in. 'Got into bother last nicht for goin' too hard roon thae curves,' said Poker. 'Dam't, they shouldna have as mony curves in the road.' This, as my friend Marshall remarked, was really getting down to basic causes. If an inspector was sent to investigate, Poker would drop about 10 minutes on schedule. Finally they sent *two* investigators, Joe Jardine, the locomotive inspector and John McCrae the assistant shed foreman. That trip was another classic. Poker was tearing down those hills. Jardine, who was nervous, was sitting over on the fireman's side and was shouting 'Canny on there! Canny on!', while McCrae, standing behind the driver was saying, 'Go on, Erchie! Let her have it!'

No 14518 was not really a very good one. I thought her slow on the hill. By 1927 four of Ayr's Drummonds had been superheated – Nos 14510/13–15 (ex-331/4–6, ex-131/4–6). No 14514 was the best of the bunch, doing a lot of work on the 3.55pm in summer and the 4.10pm in winter. On 28 July 1927 Poker Ross had this locomotive on the Paddy with a load of about 280 tons full. He had a pilot to Girvan, which was reached in 58 minutes (72 booked), then single-handed ran Girvan-Ayr in 28 minutes, with a stop at Maybole. (25 minutes' late start from Stranraer Harbour, 10 minutes late at Ayr.)

There is no doubt that the Stranraer road at that period was far from safe for one of those Drummond engines. There were many soft spots, and the LMS methods of superelevation of curves which transformed this road in after years had scarcely begun in 1927. There were some alarming experiences. Geordie Thomson of Girvan was coming down from the Chirmorie to Barrhill with No 14521 on the 4.15pm ex-Stranraer. As the train entered the Gunner's Cut No 14521 gave a furious lurch, and from beneath the bogie came 'a thing like three smiddy-fires'. Geordie thought she had gone off the road and back on. So did I, but more than 30 years later I read in *The Railway Magazine* for November 1960 (page 798) the testimony of a man who had been a fitter at Salisbury in 1906. 'All the L&SW top-link drivers were certain they knew the cause of the accident.' This was the derailment of the up boat-train at Salisbury on 1 July 1906. 'The means of lubrication provided on the larger 4–4–0s to afford free play between the bogie and mainframe were hopelessly inadequate and at times the bogie would "bind" and as a result violent lurches and swings would occur.' When the damaged engine was rerailed, this fitter was instructed to lubricate thoroughly the surfaces between the bogie and the main frame. 'Improved lubrication between these parts was quietly provided on all the larger 4–4–0s as they underwent major shopping; this transformed their riding and cured the sudden "binding" previously experienced.'

To my way of thinking, this is most important information. Not only does it throw light upon the immediate cause of the Salisbury derailment, but it offers a solution of the problems of the bad riding of the Drummond 4–4–0s of the G&SW. Take the case of Geordie Thomson. The bogie slides *seized* just as they took the sharp curve into the Gunner's Cut. The whole engine was thrown violently sideways as it hit the curve. Then the slides burst free in a blaze of fire. 'Sudden' and 'unexpected' – these were the predominant words of G&SW drivers who described those experiences. I gathered that one day a Drummond would negotiate a curved bit of road in perfect style, the next day there would be a violent stagger and a threatened overturning. 'You have to watch them. You never know the minute . . .' they would say.

Now I never heard this theory expressed concerning the G&SW Drummonds. I never heard that authority took any cognizance of those happenings. I can only say that complaints became fewer in number as time went on. I attributed this to the improved state of the track. I wonder now if the LMS authorities solved the problem and provided a remedy. Remembering the LMS attitude to the non-standard engines, I have my doubts.

2
Per Ardua . . .

At the time of Grouping, the G&SW was probably the worst equipped of all the constituent companies for the working of its main line expresses. Those, the through trains to and from England, were still referred to as 'The Pullman', though Pullman cars had not been run on them for over 40 years. The power available for working those trains was non-superheated 4–6–0s of Manson's design, plus the two superheated ones, Nos 512/13 (ex-128/9). I know there were seven superheated Drummond 4–4–0s, but owing to heating troubles nobody would trust them on the Pullman jobs. The 4–6–4 Baltic tanks did not have enough water-carrying capacity. The Manson 4–6–0s had been good engines in their day, but by the end of the first world war they were badly run-down. As they passed through the shops Whitelegg fitted each one with an extended smokebox. The 4–6–0s promptly refused to steam, so in desperation there was fitted to the back of the blastpipe a 'razor' (English enginemen would call it a 'jimmy'). This could be lowered across the blastpipe by a crank and a rod from the cab. Drivers had been using this device on bad-steaming engines for years, but in secret. It was nearly the sack if they were found out – it was *bad* for the engines . . . Now authority was using it officially. There were a few sardonic comments.

So the Pullman men were not getting on very well – non-superheated engines on a main line job in 1923. Carlisle men were working those trains as far as Kilmarnock. Hurlford men took over for the steep grades of the Barrhead road into Glasgow. They had one Baltic tank, No 545, which did a morning and an evening trip into Glasgow, together with two 4–6–0s which did less important turns, and deputised for the Baltic during its frequent

21

absences in Kilmarnock shops for heating.

The Carlisle men had the two superheated 4–6–0s at this time, but they did not seem to make much of a mark. They also had Nos 510/11 (ex-126/7) which had the longer firebox, and Whitelegg's fancy cab. They did not seem to be much good, either. E. C. Poultney had a footplate run on No 510 and he described it in *The Engineer* dated 12 November 1920. It was not a brilliant performance. He said that the fireman had to work very hard. Except on the descent of the two banks (from Stewarton and from New Cumnock), ten to twelve shovelfuls were fired every two minutes. No 510 was a bit unfortunate. There was a blow-off cock under the firehole. A movement of the cab tore off the cock one day, and driver Peter Finlinson was terribly burned. Then on 3 November 1924 (she was No 14672 by then) Jack Irving had her on the 9.20am from Glasgow. They were just approaching Auldgirth when the left-hand bottom slide-bar dropped. The connecting rod broke and dug into the ground. Fortunately it struck a soft place and came round to the trailing position without heaving her over.

Things were not very happy on the Pullman jobs, but there was no great rush on the part of the other LMS constituents to help. The G&SW had the two superheated express engines, the Caley had 79! Yet not one came to the G&SW section. Certainly the Caley diverted its night sleeper, the 11.45pm ex-Euston, to run via the G&SW route, hauled by a Caley engine, but that was purely to help the Caley. For years this 11.45pm had been a nuisance, a heavy train, blundering into the path of The Tinto, that train by which the Caley set great store. This move got rid of it. G&SW men had to pilot it from Dumfries.

Early in LMS days, a strange working was put on from Carlisle. A G&SW driver with a non-superheated 4–6–0 took one of the night trains to St Enoch in the morning, then he went round to Central and worked the 10.00am back to Carlisle by the Caley road. The G&SW man got no conductor from Central, but was always piloted throughout by a Caley engine. I can only think that this was to teach the Caley road to the G&SW men. This working kept on for some years – by 1925 the pilot was frequently a Kingmoor compound.

The Baltic at Hurlford gave a lot of trouble. Bogie boxes were a pest. When John McNallie had her he was buying castor oil to try to cure the heating! She was good on the uphill, but coming down you had to watch her. They tell of one day when old Will Wallace was letting her rip a bit down Stewarton. She gave one of her victory rolls and the fireman cries 'Canny on, Willie!' Old Willie was religious. He says 'Boy, I'm no' fiert. I am Prepared to Go.' 'Aweel', says the fireman, 'I'm no' Prepared. Pit the brakes on her!'

Oh, they were terrors at times. The Corkerhill Baltic, No 543, had a sort of permanent job on the 4.10pm to Stranraer, which she took as far as Girvan. One day someone in authority–some say Whitelegg himself–went down on the footplate to Girvan. After sampling her performance on the reverse curves down from Maybole, authority had No 543 warned off the course and limited to Ayr turns only. So they gave her the 5.15pm to Ayr, returning on the 9.20pm semi-fast–very semi. Sanny Colquhoun was driving No 543 at that time, and his fireman was Jimmy McBride, a big craggy individual whom all at Corkerhill called 'Gus'. On the 9.20pm one night, old Sanny had gone away down the street at Ayr, and Gus started to get some coal in. Gus liked to get plenty into the firebox then put up his feet and enjoy the drive, so he shovelled and shovelled till the coal got a bit beyond his reach. He looked into the bunker–there was only about a barrowful left. Gus thought it a pity to leave it out in the cold, so he put it in too, shut the firedoor and let it cook. About 9.15pm old Sanny comes along. Gus says, 'We've done it tonight, old timer! We've done it tonight! Look, no coal!' Old Sanny nearly passed out. No coal! Gus had enough in the firebox to take the train to Perth!

They missed No 543 on the 4.10pm, for she could take 300 tons south of Ayr, and the 4.10pm could be a heavy train. From the summer of 1923, Ayr men took on the 4.10pm south of Ayr, going through to Stranraer and back with the Paddy at 9.25pm.

With the restrictions on the PP&W, the heaviest locomotive that Ayr could provide were Manson's 18 class 4 – 4 – 0s. Nos 338/40 (ex-26/8) were put on this job. Good engines in their day, but their motion had been altered to the Whitelegg design and that, together with the usual sleeping pill, had sapped their energy sadly. Jimmy Aitken and Jimmy Hannah got the job. Hannah used to look across at night to the Muirkirk men with their splendid No 1060 and shout 'I'll swop you!' Hannah had an unfortunate mishap before he had been long on that job. There was not much time to spare from getting to the shed at Stranraer till they had to be off to take the train down to the harbour for The Paddy. Stranraer men would buckle in and help. That night one was cleaning the fire, two were getting coal forward, another was carrying sand—and they forgot to fill the tank! The injector blew off at Glenwhilly . . . it was very bad luck. Another $4\frac{1}{2}$ miles and they would have been over the top and could have drifted down to Barrhill and filled up.

So 1923 passed with no improvement in motive power for passenger services. It was the autumn of 1924 before rumours began to circulate of *new engines* of LMS design coming to the G&SW section. Better late than never. In October they arrived . . . shunting tanks! Why, no one knew. We were not needing them as we had plenty of shunters. The North British Locomotive Company was turning out a big batch for the LMS, and they were being distributed around the sheds like advertisements for soap powder. Hurlford got three; Ayr got three, Nos 7132-4. They were 0–6–0 side tanks, obviously of Midland extraction. Our men were interested. Here were the first engines designed and approved by the new company. They examined them; they returned shocked. 'My God!' said a driver to me, 'They're like something George Stephenson left ower!'

They were truly terrible. The first thing that caught the eye was the lever reverse; we had had power reverse on our engines since 1875. There was only one gauge glass; we had had duplicate glasses since 1879. The firedoor was an incomprehensible affair of plates and ratchets and chains. But – the supreme iniquity –

you could not lean out and watch your shunter while handling the regulator. On the G&SW, that was a *sine qua non*, and here, on these awful machines, you had to lose sight of your shunter and take two or three steps across the footplate to work this wretched little upright handle. This was what this new company considered an engine with all mod cons. Faith was sadly shaken.

I have seen it written that it was the G&SW men who christened those engines *Jinties*. As far as I am concerned, I never heard the term used. I do not think that the G&SW men used any such intimate term for those engines. Their scorn was too great.

This was, however, the breaking of the ice. By early 1925, I was hearing of Midland-type superheated 0–6–0s working on main line goods to Glasgow. At St Enoch shed, in from Carlisle, I saw Nos 4178, 4180 and 4181. I did not, however, get a close look at them; in fact throughout their sojourn on G&SW territory, I never had much experience of those engines or their work. Then in July my grapevine telegraph, working a little sluggishly, reported that Midland compounds had been working from Carlisle to St Enoch for about a month. These happenings were rather out of my orbit just then. I saw No 1065 outside St Enoch shed, and I saw Jack Irving The Craw, boarded two minutes late off Carlisle, come into Kilmarnock with No 1069 eight minutes early, which seemed to betoken good work. Of course I had read of the Settle & Carlisle trials by that time, and was not surprised.

Then in October 1925 we got more new engines. These were Caley-designed 0–4–4Ts, with some augmentations that Pickersgill had added – 18¼in cylinders and 180lb/sq in boiler pressure. The LMS had just had ten of those built by Nasmyth, Wilson. Three came to our district. Ayr got Nos 15260/1, and Dalmellington No 15262 – surely the first, and last, *new* engine to come to our little sub-shed.

The reception of those engines was quite different from that of the shunters. They had Caley fittings, of course, but Drummond had in a measure prepared us for those. They had the Westinghouse brake on the engine, but so had our older engines of Smellie's era. The only real snag was the lever reverse. It was murderously stiff to work. Our men wrestled with it for a week or two until one day in desperation one of them slacked back the nuts on the top of the plummer blocks, whereupon you could pull it over with one hand!

No 15262 had not been very long at Dalmellington when she was involved in a most extraordinary happening. She was on the 6.40am empty coaches Dalmellington to Rankinston. The crews were a bit disorganised that morning. Craig was ill, and a passed fireman from Ayr was deputising. Craig's fireman had swopped with Smith's fireman, an elderly man who had never progressed to driving. They got to Holehouse Junction and were held up there, Rankinston being late in opening. Presently, however, the signalman got the tablet. He did not bother to pull off the branch home signal, but ran down the long stair, gave them the tablet, and said 'Right!' Off they went.

Now No 15262 was a splendid engine, but the crew should have been really astonished at the way she went up that 1 in 80 to Rankinston. Still, at 7 o'clock on a cold, dark November morning you are not at your best for assessing locomotive performance. They were content to snuggle into their warm cab and let the black world outside go by. But presently a yellow light showed momentarily through the back window. Strange. Then two red lights, side-by-side, then the dim lighted windows of a signalbox! Where on earth . . .? They were past them all before they could gather their wits. They were not on the Rankinston line at all — they were on the *Ayr* line, past Hollybush station, past Potterston box, almost at the viaduct. By the mercy of Providence the 6.39am passenger from Ayr was late that morning, or they would have been head-on into it. The Holehouse signalman had never set the road for Rankinston.

There was a desperate rush back up to Holehouse, then away to Rankinston. Then the inquiry, where nothing could be hushed up, and there was an awful row. The Holehouse signalman was demoted to be porter at Hollybush. The driver got 14 days' suspension, the fireman seven, the guard three, which was rather hard on the guard, for he was the only one who had sensed something wrong. He had put down his window and looked out, but they were in a cutting, which corresponded to the Rankinston road. Even the Potterston signalman had done wrong, for he had allowed them to return to Holehouse without a Potterston/Holehouse tablet. Truly a bad business all round.

It would be about the end of 1925 that the Control system came to our part of the country. Circuit telephones were installed and a control centre established at Kilmarnock station. Kilmarnock Control did some good work in later years, but it will be understood that, with this new organisation starting from scratch, not all of the staff would be fully conversant with the geography of the district. There were many tales of ignorance and inefficiency. One concerned a derailment on the single line near New Luce. The stationmaster reported it to Control, and was told to open single-line working . . .!

The year 1926 was largely overshadowed by the strikes, the general strike and the long coal strike which followed. Railway working in our district was much upset, with services curtailed or suspended and, after the general strike, enginemen working a three-day week. Unfamiliar engines appeared. The Pumpers, with no coal trains to haul, came up on the Dalmellington goods, or 'freight', as we now had to call it. I remember one day No 17755 was on it, with Andy Gilchrist and Harry Barr. It was a bit cold to go back to Ayr tender-first, so they decided to turn her. The Pumpers were still the heaviest 0–6–0s in Britain, and our old turntable fairly groaned. We started to turn her, got about a third of the way round, and stuck, and there we were, with our train on the main line, and the passenger due in 20 minutes! I ran to the station, but could find only one porter. Then to the goods shed, where I got the station carter and his two sons, and the seven of us laid at it. 'Get her back to the straight,' Gilchrist called. Toodley Barr and I were pushing at the back. The Drummond tenders had a great overhang at the rear, and I was right in below it, with grim thoughts of what would happen if that centre-casting broke! When we got back to the straight it was going fast. 'Keep her going,' Gilchrist cries. 'She'll maybe go right round.' With one terrific WOOOMPH over the bit where we had stuck we turned her successfully, but I would rather not be at the turning of another!

It was at this time that someone with little knowledge sent a Pumper round the Dunure and Maidens line with the daily goods. This was always referred to as a light railway, and it was — after the Pumper had gone over it there were eleven broken rails!

Of course, coal began to run short, and I was at Ayr sheds the day the first American coal arrived. A Whitelegg rebuild, No 14163 (ex-416, ex-75) was going on the Stranraer run. It received three hutches of coal from the bing and three of American. It was hardly better than powder, and all mixed up with straw, to prevent breakage; the tender was like a farmyard. 'Yankee duff' the men called it. Some of it was not so bad, it was good enough coal but soft. For the first time we got automatic stokers . . . If there was a chip out of the firedoor and you held a shovelful of this duff to the opening the draught would suck it in. But they were getting coal from many sources, and some was just terrible. Sam Sproat and Jackie Cameron had one of Smellie's 0–6–0s rebuilt by Manson, No 149 (ex-291). They booked on and got a train of empties at Ayr harbour to take to Burnockhill pit, where there was some coal stored, 14 miles away. I do not know how many times they stuck, but by the time they got to Burnockhill their eight hours were up!

I remember Sam McKnight of Girvan telling me about sticking on the Swan's Neck one night in 1926 coming back with the goods from Stranraer. Sanny Williamson The Maltee was fireman, and he was up in the tender pecking like a hen and he could hardly get a piece the size of a golf ball. They had No 17202 that night, which did not help matters. I believe she was the very last of Whitelegg's infamous rebuilds, carried out in July 1929 – I expect the LMS was merely using up the material. No 17202 was useless, hopeless and helpless, but someone discovered that it was quite good in reverse gear. (Girvan men said the chimney was at the wrong end.) She was withdrawn from service in August 1929, surely the shortest career on record for one of those quite expensive rebuilds.

Mineral jobs were all upside down that year, working coal *from*, instead of *to* the ports. Alf Watt had gone to Kingmoor shed in 1924 with his G&SW companions, and in 1926 he was driving a Manson 4–6–0, No 14658 (ex-497, ex-383). He was booked out one day to take a train to Leeds, and was told to take his own engine. He was given a train of 50 wagons of Yankee coal. Costello, of Durranhill, came on with him as conductor, and Scott of Durranhill piloted with a Midland Class 2P 4–4–0. Costello told Alf to drive, and he would watch the signals. He stood behind Alf and every now and then he would call 'Back board. Back board.' Alf puzzled over this for a bit and then says 'What's all this *back board* business?' 'Oh,' the conductor says, 'it means you've got the distant.' Other railways, other ways.

They were relieved at Holbeck sheds by Leeds men, who were to take the train on to Hunslet. Now No 14658 had a tricky injector. When you were shutting it off the check valve would sometimes stick and it would blow back, so Alf told his fireman to warn the Leeds man. The warning was received with great rudeness. They gathered that the Leeds fireman did not need any so-and-so Carlisle man to show *him* how to work an injector. Somewhat chastened, Alf and his mate went to the office and booked-off, having been on duty 12 hours. Just then came an urgent message. An engine was waiting to rush them to Hunslet. The 4–6–0's injector had blown-back and they were getting ready to throw out the fire! They left Leeds next day on a regular goods at 10.45am piloted by the usual driver of this turn with a Class 4F 0–6–0. They gave them 100 wagons as far as Skipton and 50 from there, reaching Petteril Bridge at 6.35pm.

No 14658 must have gone to Corkerhill shortly after this trip. Bob Brown had a strange accident with her one night on the 9.20pm from Ayr. They were just approaching Brownhill Junction. Sanny Smith opened the firedoor and was coming forward with a shovelful when there was a terrific rush of steam and flame. Brown flung the regulator shut, ran along the gangway, pulled the front vacuum brake hose off the dummy, and stopped her. When he got back to the footplate the blow had stopped, the fireman was tearing off his overalls, and the place was ankle-deep in coal and firebricks. There were even ashes on the back of the tender. No 14658 had blown the whole side out of the steampipe in the smokebox, on the side next the tubeplate. Sanny Smith was rather badly burned. He told me the front pockets of his overalls were packed tightly with red-hot coal! Of course, when the regulator was shut the eruption ceased.

Several of the Kingmoor compounds were fitted for oil firing at this period. I saw nothing of their working, but I gathered that it was not too successful. They got a bit of a fright one day when a man on an oil-fired compound working a down express, the 1.00pm ex-Carlisle, ran through all signals at Eastriggs. A down local was standing in Annan station; they got all the passengers out and the signalman at Solway Junction put detonators on the line, but they stopped at Solway Junction signals. The express driver said he had been temporarily overcome by oil fumes.

Early in 1927 the Caley at last released one of its precious superheated engines for work on the G&SW section. To be truthful, it was for work on the PP&W, on which there was still an admixture of ex-Caley staff. Since the first world war, the boat trains on the PP&W had been run by G&SW Carlisle men. They had Manson 4–4–0s of the big-boilered 240 class, and they needed a lot of piloting. So LMS No 14431 (ex-Caley 769) was sent to Kingmoor for this job. It was a Dunalastair II, one of the four rebuilt with superheater, engines with an excellent reputation. On 21 April 1927 she was on the 3.13am Carlisle to Stranraer with two ex-G&SW men, Billy Wilson and Willie Nugent. As they started away from Annan, on went the vacuum brake and they stopped. Wilson shut off hurriedly and he and the fireman ran back to investigate. As they were not on speaking terms, each went up his own side. Attached to the engine were the London van and the Stranraer postal sorting carriage. They had broken away in front of the Newcastle coach. They examined the vacuum bag on the postal and it seemed all right; they put it on the dummy, then turned to see the other. Presently there was a movement and they turned to see the rear of the postal carriage vanishing into the darkness behind 14431. What to do? Cummertrees signal box was out at that time of morning; they got Ruthwell. The signalman at Ruthwell was one Alexander Brown, truly a man of enterprise. He bolted along to the platform and presently out of the night came No 14431, going slowly and getting short of breath. As she passed, Brown grabbed the cab rail, swung aboard and stopped her.

No 14431 did not seem to make much of a mark on the PP&W. A Caley engine and G&SW men, I fancy. To me, the Carlisle men never seemed to be at home on the PP&W. In the 1930s, Stranraer men got the jobs back, with Pickersgill 4—4—0s, and seemed to do better.

In common with other Scottish railways, the G&SW had never operated a Sunday passenger service. Night expresses to and from England, and connections from Kilmarnock to Ayr and Largs were about the sum total. But with the LMS, directed from London, ideas were different. Also, bus companies were springing up right left and centre, most of them with Sunday services as good or better than weekday ones. So in 1925 Sunday services were started on the Ayrshire lines, to Ayr and Girvan and to Largs. Until 1927, however, there had been no attempt to go south of Girvan.

With the bogey of Sunday rates of pay, the LMS Northern Division ran those Sunday services on a veritable shoestring. Only Glasgow Central station was used, and one locomotive depot, Polmadie. Signal boxes were switched out wherever possible. From Paisley to Kilwinning, there was no box open except Glengarnock No 2, which was kept open for the ironworks. Staffs at stations were the minimum.

In June 1927 the LMS took a really daring decision, advertising a *Sunday Excursion* from Glasgow to Portpatrick on 19 June from Central station. The G&SW men had been complaining that they were getting no share of the Sunday jobs, so authority said to Corkerhill, 'Here you are. Run this excursion to Portpatrick. Put on two of the heaviest engines which are permitted, and give the job to your two senior passenger men.' So

Corkerhill chose two big-boilered Manson 4–4–0s, Nos 14374 (ex-346, ex-157) and 14261 (ex-389, ex-259), of the 18 and 240 classes respectively. They gave them to the two oldest drivers, Sanny Rowan and Dick Gaw, who had been leading a quiet life on the 'old men's jobs'. They did not know the road into Central, but they were told to proceed to West Street and they would get a conductor from there. So they set off from Corkerhill tender-first, and with a bit of juggling got to West Street. No conductor there. 'Go on. He's at Larkfield,' said the signalman, 'It's not far.' So they got down to Larkfield, and of course landed in Central nose first! They had to come back out to Eglinton Street to turn. They got back in to find a train of eleven corridors and a Pullman diner, *Helen Macgregor*, 366 tons tare and filling rapidly.

They got away eight minutes late and sat for 15 minutes at Paisley waiting on the Largs train clearing Glengarnock. By the time the train left Paisley it was estimated that there were 950 passengers aboard. They called at Irvine, Troon and Prestwick, with a draw-up at each to let all the train get to the platforms. At Ayr, both engines took water. By this time the train was packed. There was an extra stop to pick up a party from Kilkerran. At Girvan both locomotives took water again. Webster was guard and he came forward at Girvan grumbling about the delay. Dick Gaw, flourishing his oil can, chased him up the platform, threatening to knock the bluidy heid off him.

Now came the problem. The scheduled top load for each of those engines, Girvan to Pinmore, was 140 tons, and they had 366! No assistance was available. How they got up, I shall never know. I think the regulators must have been twice round. Stop at Pinmore – another party to lift – missed the tablet at New Luce and had to stop and run back for it, arriving 80 minutes late Stranraer. They then took the whole train down to Portpatrick, rounded it (on a loop which held, I think, eight coaches) and hauled the whole lot back up to Stranraer, tender-first. At Stranraer there was nobody on duty except a signalman. They had to turn, water and coal both engines; two big fires to clean. Then they had to turn to and fill diner tanks and lavatory tanks, and by buckets, for the hoses were either locked up or could not be found. Then back down to Portpatrick, with a 40-minute late start on the return journey. They had a special stop at Dunragit, took water at both Barrhill and Girvan, stopped to set down the parties at Pinmore and Kilkerran, and had double stops at all stations except Ayr, finally arriving 148 minutes late in Glasgow Central. The engine crews booked off at Corkerhill after eighteen hours on duty!

'Splendid!' said Head Office, examining the passenger returns on Monday morning, and it promptly arranged for another similar excursion on Sunday 26 June 1927. Corkerhill took no chances this time, putting on two Drummond 4–4–0s, Nos 14519 and 14516, with two men in the prime of life who knew the road well. Result, time-and-time all day with a 345-ton train, moderately filled. But I wonder what the civil engineer said when he heard that two Drummonds coupled together had been down that poor little line to Portpatrick. They were lucky to get back, but I never heard of another Drummond venturing south of Stranraer again.

3

Compounds and 2Ps

On 24 June 1924, by order of the LMS, the G&SW shed at Currock, Carlisle was closed and its engines and men removed almost by force to the much grander establishment of the Caledonian at Kingmoor. It was not a happy move. The G&SW men did not want to leave Currock, and the Kingmoor men hated the sight of them. A year later, in 1925, there was little sign of integration, each tribe keeping to its former duties on its former territory.

That was the situation when in the early summer of 1925 there came to Kingmoor that phenomenal windfall, 20 LMS compound 4—4—0s. What prompted it, no one knew. The Caley was sitting very pretty with something like 25 superheated engines for its express turns. The G&SW was in extreme need, but it seemed hardly possible that news of this could have been allowed to reach the ears of those in Euston. But the compounds came, the sheep carefully divided from the goats. The Caley got 15, brand new from the North British Locomotive Co, and driven from the left-hand side, as was official Caley practice. No one seems to have told Euston that as soon as a Caley crew got away on a run of any length, the driver crossed to the right-hand side and the fireman fired from the left.

Five compounds formed the G&SW portion, very considerately, right-hand drive engines off the Midland Division, Nos 1065—9. Even so, we were bereft of two, for 1066/7 were wanted for duties down south, so the Caley had to part with two of its contingent. The G&SW link was No 1065 Jack Maxwell, No 1068 Tom Harrison, No 1069 Jack Irving, No 1137 Jimmy Fraser, and No 1149 Tommy Gibbons. As soon as they settled

Above: LMS No 14666, Manson 4-6-0 ex G&SW 119/505.
British Railways Board

Below: LMS No 15401, Whitelegg 4-6-4T ex G&SW 541.
J. H. L. Adams

Above: LMS No 14369, Manson 18 class 4-4-0 ex G&SW 28/340.
D. L. Smith collection

Below: Stranraer train leaving Glasgow (St Enoch); LMS No 15405, Whitelegg 4-6-4T ex G&SW 545.
Photomatic Ltd

down, the practice of changing engines at Kilmarnock was abolished. Carlisle men worked to Glasgow and back on one shift, and Corkerhill got a similar turn, the 12.00 midday to Carlisle, back on the 4.21pm ex Carlisle.

Of course, Corkerhill had no compounds. Kingmoor sent them back their two Manson 4–6–0 superheaters, but they did not seem to have benefited from the air of the Borders, and were often laid up for various ailments. So the engine for the 12.00pm was more usually a non-superheated 4–6–0.

A link of four very able drivers had this midday job – Jock Paterson had No 14669, Bob Brown No 14658, while Sam Mitchell and Fred Hough had, officially, superheaters Nos 14673 and 14674 respectively. This was the link which became well known in after years as the Big Four. They did their best on the train, but it was a struggle. One could only hope that another influx of modern material might take place, but the Caley was sitting prettier than ever, and there was no one to plead the cause of the G&SW. Nearly two more years went by; things were getting very bad. An entry in my notebook dated 10 February 1927 reads:

> 14671 and 14672 are at Hurlford. 14658 at Corkerhill ran up a big end very badly on the Pullman and off to shops for a new crankpin. 14671 sent in place, but found bogie framing broken, so 14672 sent. In wretched order. Takes about 53 minutes, [schedule 47 minutes] pounded unmercifully to pass New Cumnock from Dumfries.

In April 1927, we heard that new compounds were coming to Scotland! They were from Vulcan Foundry, numbered 900 upwards – help at last. Polmadie received Nos 900–9. Quite right – Corkerhill would be next, say another ten. Here was the distribution: Nos 910/11 Fairlie Pier, No 912 Ardrossan, Nos 913/14 Corkerhill, Nos 915/16 Hurlford . . .

Fifty-three years later I can still find no rational explanation of that crazy distribution. Fairlie Pier was a three-engine sub-shed already equipped with two Baltic tanks; Hurlford had no express turns at all, while Corkerhill, so desperately needing help –

received *two*. No 913 went to Jock Paterson and No 914 to Bob Brown. The 12.00pm, of course, became easy meat, the only trouble being that when Mitchell or Hough were on it, they had to borrow a compound, which did not make for harmony. With the winter timetable of 1927, the Big Four were given a great boost to morale. A new train was going on, the 1.50pm Glasgow Central to Liverpool and Manchester, with one stop at Strawfrank Junction (Carstairs) to attach the Edinburgh portion. The Corkerhill Big Four were to work this train to Carlisle, returning on the 6.34pm from Carlisle by the G&SW road.

All four had to learn the Caley road. In their absence, younger men appeared on various Big Four turns. I used to see them on the 7.00am to Girvan and 11.30am back. All were keenly interested in compounds and delighted to get a chance to work them. Jock Douglas vowed that he could start away in compound, in defiance of what the book said. He gave me a demonstration, leaving Ayr. He put the regulator 'right over' and it certainly started all right, but with a fore-and-aft surge for a bit before the speed got up. I suppose that one really could not put the handle over quickly enough to avoid a little live steam getting into the low-pressure cylinder, enough to set the locomotive in motion. Douglas said that one morning he did that at every start from Glasgow to Girvan and back, 42 of them, and the locomotive refused only once, at Dailly northbound, where the start was right on to a 1 in 70 grade.

Another of those younger men was Will Scott, son of Bob Scott of Girvan, the ex-Wheatley man. When Will Scott went first to Corkerhill, he was injudicious enough to state that the moon was bigger at Girvan than it was at Corkerhill. Thereafter he was always referred to as 'the Big Min'. He was on 914 in place of Bob Brown one day, and he took me on the footplate to Troon to get my opinion on an intermittent blow from the right-hand low-pressure piston. Having been thus elevated to the position of consulting engineer I solemnly gave Scott a written report with my opinion; it turned out to be the correct solution, which was rather wonderful.

So the Big Four went on to the 1.50pm turn, and presently I was being regaled with stories of the big loads they were taking over Beattock summit, and of their grand sprints home with the 6.34pm. The latter was usually fairly light, but frequently a bit late off the Midland, and quite a lot of this lateness could be recovered. It was an interesting period, for the Manson superheaters had had a good overhaul, so Mitchell and Hough got them on the 1.50pm and 6.34pm and they did very well indeed. I have a note of five runs on the 6.34pm and append a summary table of them, giving *net* times, in minutes, throughout.

Date		25.10.27	24.2.28	1.3.28	2.4.28	7.4.28
Engine No		913	14673	14673	914	14674
Driver		Hough	Mitchell	Mitchell	Brown	Hough
Fireman		Cook	Sharp	Sharp	Gibson	Cook
Load (tare – tons)		187	192	187	201	259
Late start (mins)		31	17	25	11	—

	Schedule (mins)		Actual times (minutes)			
Carlisle–Dumfries	41	33	35	35	35½	36
Dumfries–New Cumk (pass)	45	38	41	42	41¼	42¼
Dumfries–Kilmarnock	69	57	60	61	62¼	62¼
Kilmarnock–St Enoch	38	30	31	32	—	32¼
Late arrival (mins)		10	3	10	4½	—

The Kilmarnock–St Enoch schedule allows for a conditional call at Strathbungo. This call was made on the fifth run only. Net time is the equivalent of a non-stop run.

Fred Hough's run with No 14674 was a fine piece of work, and a great tribute to that great engine, the famous No 129. In June 1928 a friend took me to visit James Manson, the only time that I ever met him. I gave him a detailed copy of this run, and he was greatly pleased. Later that year, Manson attended a gathering in Corkerhill Hall. There was much laudatory speaking concerning the fine work being done by modern LMS engines. Manson said that he quite agreed, but – here he produced the log I had given him – 'I have here a document which shows that our own old engines can still hold their own with the new ones of today.' Fred Hough, in the audience, joined heartily in the applause.

Alas, the Indian summer of the Manson superheaters was of short duration. In May 1928 ten more compounds came to Scotland. Two came to Corkerhill. Mitchell got No 1179 and Hough No 1180. Nos 1181/2 went to Ayr. So the Big Four all got compounds, and the summer of 1928 saw them rarin' to go. I was particularly anxious to get them on to the Stranraer road, and when the summer rosters came out the compounds were detailed to take the 3.55pm through to Stranraer, returning on the Paddy . . . and they gave the job to the second link!

I had no objection to the second link; they were good men — Adam Craven, John Calder, Geordie Gilchrist and Jimmy Scott, whom they called 'Trencher'. But they had little or no experience of compounds, and as we found out very soon, a compound on the Stranraer road could be a handful, due to their slipping. We had thought that the Drummond 4—4—0s were bad for slipping, but they could not hold a candle to the compounds. Weather conditions on the Stranraer line could pose problems enough, but in addition the LMS had been canting the curves for higher speeds downhill. Comfort at speed had improved out of all knowledge, but a compound, struggling uphill at 20mph was helped not at all by the curve being canted over for an engine coming downhill at 60mph. On 11 June 1928 I was at Girvan station when the 3.55pm came in with John Calder and No 1180. Calder did not know the road south of Girvan, so Jock Hannah was waiting to conduct him. Neither Calder nor Hannah had been on a compound before. Calder's comments on the situation, delivered in his strong Caithness accent, were very pithy. They worked away most of the summer, but more often than not the compounds were taken for other jobs and the second link men were back with their Drummond superheater 4—4—0s, Nos 14516/7/9/20 which they had had before. Better the devil they knew than the one they did not!

On 10 September 1928 Scott was on the Paddy with No 14517. Harry Kennedy, that merry-faced lad, was firing. They passed through Pinwherry station, and Harry leaned out to bring in the tablet-catcher. The door swung open as the locomotive took the curve, and Harry fell out. They stopped, and got him up into the train. One of the dining car staff went on the footplate to Girvan, where they got another fireman. Harry was pretty badly hurt and was off work for a while.

There seemed to be a jinx about Pinwherry that summer. Two months before, at the very spot where Harry fell out, two of his mates from Corkerhill met their end. It happened on the Stranraer goods, not the wild 1.00am but its return trip, the 6.30pm from Stranraer, which seldom conveyed more than a single engine load and ran decorously and apparently without difficulty. With the summer workings at Corkerhill, there was a shift-up, and Tom Robson went on to the link which ran this duty. Robson was an experienced and most reliable man, but he did not know the road south of Girvan, so for five trips he travelled with Will Scott. On the fifth trip, Scott allowed Robson to handle the engine, which he did to Scott's entire satisfaction. On all five trips, the engine was No 17759, accounted one of the best of the Drummond 0–6–0s at Corkerhill. On 2 June Robson did the Stranraer trip without a conductor in a satisfactory manner.

On 2 July he was again rostered for the 1.00am. For this Robson asked for, and was given, No 17759. The fireman, Tommy Rennick, had been with Robson since early June, but not on a Stranraer trip. Rennick had seven years' firing experience. The guard was Johnnie Maule of St John's, who had long experience of the Stranraer road, and had been on this turn since its inception. He knew Robson well, and at the subsequent inquiry spoke of him as 'an extra good driver'.

The 1.00am was run without incident. The three men booked off at Stranraer and went to lodgings, booking-on again for the 6.30pm. No 17759 was prepared for the 6.30pm by Andrew McCreadie of Stranraer, a careful and reliable man. When Robson came on duty, he talked with McCreadie; the two of them tested the vacuum brake and found all in order. They left at 6.25pm, five minutes early, with 24 wagons and brake van. At

Dunragit they picked up five more, making 29, equal to 31. The maximum load for a Drummond was 32 loaded goods wagons. A fitted van was coupled to the engine. There was ample brake power to control a train of this weight.

They got to Glenwhilly at 7.41pm and were held 31 minutes to cross the 5.10pm, leaving Glenwhilly seven minutes late. From the Chirmorie, Robson made a careful descent to Barrhill, stopping correctly at the water column. There had been a shower, otherwise the evening was fine and clear. Eleven minutes were spent filling the tank. The guard came forward and talked with Robson. Everything appeared to be perfectly normal. They left at 8.44pm three minutes late.

The guard said that it was usual to start the train out of Barrhill, then to shut off steam. Then about half-way to Pinwherry, the engine brakes would be applied, and he would apply his van brake. On this night he felt no braking from the engine. Instead, the whistle was sounded, and continued for a long way. He put his brake full on, but speed continued to rise. He began to doubt if they could get through Pinwherry safely, and braced himself for a crash. Pinwherry was no place for high speed, being the worst on the road. Just short of the signalbox the line curved alongside the down platform at 20 chains radius, then came an eight-chain twist into the straight at the end of the loop, while just through the overbridge the line swung right again at an average of 20 chains. Passage through all loops between Girvan and Challoch Junction was at that time restricted to 15mph. In the case of Pinwherry this was probably justified. Certainly in the past trains had come through Pinwherry at far higher speeds, but the engines were light 4–4–0s. A 57-ton 0–6–0, with a rigid wheelbase of 17ft 1in was a different proposition altogether.

At 8.44pm, Paul Fairbairn, signalman at Pinwherry, got 'train-entering-section' from Barrhill. He obtained a tablet from Pinmore, hung it on the catcher, and crossed to the station buildings on the up platform. A relief clerk, Hugh McKail, was working in the office. Presently there was heard the long, continuous whistle. Signalman and clerk went out on to the up platform to see what was the matter. The stationmaster, in his house above the office, went to his front window. The goods train came in sight, travelling very fast. The whistling stopped as it approached the signalbox, then the train tore through the station. At the north end of the loop the engine rocked wildly, probably derailed, and just beyond the overbridge plunged down the banking, turned upside down, and ploughed into the soft earth, bursting through a stone dyke. Twenty-five wagons piled in after it. Clouds of steam burst forth; the wheels continued to revolve for some minutes. Driver and fireman were killed instantly. The guard was unhurt, but sorely shaken and shocked.

The whole line was shocked. What had gone wrong? Why should this happen, with all conditions favourable? They got the engine hauled up and conducted a thorough examination. There was no defect to account for the accident. There had been nothing unusual in the routine of the footplate. The tablet had been exchanged and the Pinmore tablet taken into the cab, all just as usual. The engine when first seen had not been steaming, but the driver had evidently applied steam just before the crash. It was a pity that no one was on the down platform at Pinwherry. Of the watchers on the up side, only McKail claimed to have seen anything of the footplatemen. At the Fatal Accidents Inquiry he said that 'there was no indication from the driver that anything was wrong, but I saw him with his hand up, as if releasing the whistle.'

On 12 July the inquiry on behalf of the Minstry of Transport was held at Pinwherry. Colonel A. C. Trench, the inspecting officer, travelled from Glasgow in the official saloon, with a number of officials and witnesses. Will Scott, with whom Robson had learned the road, was under interrogation for an hour. Colonel Trench looked somewhat doubtfully at the speed restriction of 15mph through the loops, and inquired if in fact drivers were not in the habit of exceeding this rather low figure. He was assured NO. All drivers kept rigorously to this 15mph restriction; the infringement in this accident had been quite unprecedented. The inquiry finished about 5.30pm and the officials set off on the return trip to Glasgow, but Pinmore looped them for the 3.55pm. It was a fine afternoon; while they waited, Inspector and officials went out on the end platform of the saloon. Down came the 3.55pm, a compound piloted by a small Manson 4–4–0, at a good 40 to 45mph through the loop, disappearing down the valley with a flourish of the tail van. I am told that there were some red faces among the officials on the end platform.

Colonel Trench's report came out in mid-October. I was sorely disappointed with it. It seemed to me that, like other people, he had merely shrugged his shoulders and said, 'What can I make of it?' He said, 'I can only think that the excessive speed was due to over-confidence leading to misjudgment on the part of Driver Robson . . . he forgot the severe curvature through Pinwherry and the speed restriction at this point.'

Yes, it all savoured of people saying 'What does it matter?' To me, it mattered quite a bit. A man for whom I had had a great respect was, now that he was dead, getting the blame. I heard the careless talk: 'Oh, he was just doin' a bit o' speedin' – bit o' a dasher.' I thought this was entirely wrong – a man who is doing a bit of surreptitious speeding does not start advertising the fact by blowing his whistle for a couple of miles. That whistle puzzled me. The guard said, 'It was not a whistle for me to apply the brake, as the brake whistle is given in short and sharp blasts.' Inspector Hampton of Stranraer stated, 'The long whistle was to indicate that the train could not stop at Pinwherry even in case of need.'

For a long time I pondered over the problem. Then suddenly, one day, I saw light. *The whistle* – that was the clue after all! I believe that about half-way between Barrhill and Pinwherry, just about the point at which it was usual to apply engine brakes, the crew whistled at someone or something. The whistle stuck open. Drummond whistles quite often did that. The spindle was high up near the roof of the cab, so the driver jumped up on his seat-box to try to stop the whistle; the fireman probably jumped up too. The two exasperated men struggled with the wretched thing while it squalled on, alarming the whole countryside. When they got it stopped, or maybe before, Robson got down, to find that he was well past the accustomed braking point, and that the speed had got much higher than in previous runs. He saw that he was just about Pinwherry down distant, a bit late to get the train down to the moderate speed usual at this point. And why should he? There was *some* sort of speed restriction at Pinwherry, but nobody had told him that it was as severe as 15mph. Pinwherry was in a dip. He had been taught to go fast through a dip to keep the couplings tight, so he let her go, feeling no apprehension. The tablet was exchanged and taken in; as he passed through the station Robson opened his regulator for the ensuing up-grade ... That, I believe, is what happened. We shall never know.

The summer ended, the 3.55pm came off and the 4.10pm became the Stranraer train. The Big Four got the job, right through to Stranraer, and back with the Paddy. But alas, it was not the original Big Four. For Adam Craven had claimed that he was senior to *all* in the link, so he had to get his place and poor Bob Brown, the junior man, had to go down to the second link. In after years, Adam Craven and I became great friends, but at that period I could not but feel distinctly uncharitable towards the man who had displaced my dear friend Bob Brown. Also, Craven was no runner; any time lost stayed lost; any flicker of a red signal counted three minutes added to his time. He improved a bit later. Rather strangely, Jock Paterson did not know the Stranraer road, but he learned it speedily, and did very well.

The Big Four stopped short at Ayr on Saturdays – Ayr men took the 4.10pm on and brought the Paddy back. Ayr's lately-acquired compound, No 1181, was usually sent on this job. When Ayr got its two compounds, it did not quite know what to do with them. Having recently got No 543 from Corkerhill and No 545 from Hurlford, Ayr had four Baltics and the four-cylinder 4–4–0 *Lord Glenarthur* for the Glasgow road, not to speak of four Drummonds now rebuilt with superheater. The compounds were rather dissimilar. No 1181 was always a good engine, No 1182 always a second-best. The latter had been an oil-burner during the coal strike, and was said to have suffered therefrom. Anyway, No 1181 was generally on this Saturday Stranraer turn, and on 29 December 1928 Will Kerr and Willie White had a train of 214 tons tare back with the Paddy. This was quite enough, for it was a beastly night. Up by the Swan's Neck it was blowing wet sleet. However, they were getting up. As they passed the surfacemen's hut Kerr called across to White, 'Weel, that's us by the worst!' and just at that No 1181 gave a terrific slip and stopped. They tried to get away, but she just spun with them. White got out and shovelled ashes, but she would only go up to the end of the ashes and spin again. They had to divide the train, take the first portion to Glenwhilly and come back for the second, losing 66 minutes. It was a rather painful lesson in what might be expected with the compounds on the Stranraer road. We were to become rather familiar with such happenings in the future. A week later, Kelly had No 1181 on the Paddy with 220 tons. With a dry rail, he came through on time with no bother.

The compounds may have been predominant in 1928, but the summer of that year saw the first arrivals of a class that would have an even greater influence on the old G&SW district. On 5 June I was told that a new 4-4-0 had come that morning to Hurlford shed – no, not a compound. It was painted black, and its number was 570. It was, of course, one of the earliest of the LMS version of the Midland superheater rebuilds. Later, we were to know them, from their load classification, as the 2P class. At first, the men called them 'The Wee Black Yins'.

They came not in battalions. Hurlford got four, Nos 570/1/3/4, then No 577 came solitary to Corkerhill; Ardrossan got Nos 578/9. It was rather ludicrous that only one came to Corkerhill, with not a word of instruction concerning it. Not long after she came, Corkerhill was short of a compound for the Sunday excursion to Keswick, so they gave Jock Paterson No 577 instead. They had no instructions about load limits: a compound was allowed 300 tons over the Barrhead road, No 577 was much the same *shape* as a compound, so they presumed that it would take the same load. And so Jock Paterson went away gaily with 284 tons on the Keswick. 'She's no' much worth,' he told me next day, '22 meenits t' turn the Shilford, an' I had her full open and full fore gear.' I do not suppose anyone else ever took

284 tons over Shilford with a class 2P. When the new load book came out, top load for a class 2P over this section was 170 tons! In October 1928, ten more arrived. Nos 590–2 came to Hurlford, Nos 593/4 to St Enoch, Nos 595/6 to Corkerhill, No 597 to Girvan, Nos 598/9 to Ayr. I want to say at once that those were truly great little engines. Bob Brown at Corkerhill, ousted from the Big Four, found compensation in being given the new No 595, and being also re-united with his old fireman from No 914, Mornie Gibson. The pair of them had made a grand job with No 914; they were to do splendid work on No 595 also. Corkerhill got the 5.10pm Ayr on Saturday nights. Brown and Gibson had No 595 on it on 19 January 1929 with 256 tons; with no undue exertion they were in Ayr in 48 minutes 47 seconds, allowed 50 minutes. Brown told me he kept on shortening his cut-off till he could have sworn the locomotive was getting no steam at all, and she was fairly flying. One night on the 6.20pm he thought he *had* drawn her too far up, lit the lamp and found he was running speedily forward in ten per cent of back gear!

John McDonald got No 577. I saw him come into Ayr one night with the 5.10pm. He was eight minutes late. He had been stopped three times on the Joint Line before Paisley and he had a load of 355 tons!

John McDonald – Big Shon – was a Highlandman. They tell of one morning Shon was on the 5.20am ex-St Enoch with No 577. Dailly was the last stop before Girvan and they came down past Killochan in grand style. As they swept past Bridgemill with no sign of braking, the fireman thought it was time he did something. 'Twenty-five mile an hour here, mate!' he cries. Shon had probably been nodding a bit. With one swipe of his big hand he sent the vacuum needle round to zero, and he ran the whole train, engine and four coaches, right through the station and up on to the 1 in 54. They backed to the platform and Jardine the locomotive inspector got out of the train. He says to Shon, 'We'll have no more of *that*,' to which Shon replies, 'Bad bloody rail this mornin'.'

Those locomotives were very economical. No 597 of Girvan

could run from Girvan to Glasgow and back, 126 miles, on two tons of coal, 35lb/mile. Girvan had six of the class eventually. Tom Prestly got No 643, one of the later arrivals. He told me of one Sunday when he ran the 1.30pm Girvan to Glasgow. In the train was an ex-Caley driver from Polmadie shed, who had worked a morning train to Girvan and was returning passenger. When they arrived at Glasgow Central the Polmadie man came up to No 643, jumped on the tender step and stared at the tank gauge. 'Here, sir,' he says to Prestly, 'Whaur did you tak' water comin' up there?' 'I didna tak' ony water,' answered Prestly, 'an' what's mair' – turning to the gauge – 'there's 1,500 gallons left in the tank. That's only 2,000 gallons used since Girvan.' 'Good heavens,' says the Polmadie man, 'I came doon wi' a big Caley wi' a 4,000-gallon tank, an' I had t' flee for the column at *Ayr* wi' the tank near dry!' He gazed at No 643 in awestruck fashion. 'They're needing' t' build a lot mair o' thae injins!' he opined.

Another batch of class 2P came down early in 1930. Dumfries received an allocation this time, Nos 603–5/13–16; Girvan got No 617, Stranraer Nos 618/19, Greenock (Ladyburn) Nos 620/1, Greenock (Princes Pier) Nos 622/3, Ardrossan Nos 624/5, St Enoch No 626, Stirling No 627. It was rather funny about No 627. After about a fortnight Stirling timidly inquired what they were to do with her . . . No 627 was vacuum-fitted, and all their coach sets were Westinghouse!

Those of other railways who scorned the 2Ps no doubt laughed loudly at the foolishness of sending two of these engines to Stranraer, at the extremity of two such heavily-graded lines. They would be very wrong. The 2Ps became the mainstay of the passenger traffic over both lines. When they had engines which could take 180 tons from Stranraer Harbour to Girvan in $63\frac{1}{2}$ minutes, there was not much wrong with them.

Not long after receiving No 618 and 619 I spoke to a Stranraer driver and asked how the Stranraer boys were getting on with 'The Wee Black Yins'. 'Oh man, man,' he says, 'they fairly like them! Gey near tak' them tae their bed wi' them!' This image of a little child going to bed clutching a favourite toy is really delightful.

4

Top Performance

The years 1929/30 saw the heyday of the compounds on the Stranraer road. Corkerhill's Big Four were working through to Stranraer all the year round, 3.53pm in summer, 4.10pm in winter. There was a change in personnel, however, for in July 1929 Fred Hough was appointed shift foreman at Corkerhill. This was well-deserved promotion, but my heart was sad at the loss to the footplate of yet another fine runner. On Fred's last night on the Paddy, with his trusty No 1180 and 175 tons, he ran from Stranraer Harbour to Girvan in 53 minutes. I doubt if this time could ever be beaten with a compound and 175 tons. Fred was succeeded in the link by Charlie Seivewright, a very fine man and a good engineman, but no record-breaker. The field was left open for Sam Mitchell.

Sam Mitchell and No 1179 was one of those great partnerships of driver and engine that you got from time to time in the old days. The pair became almost legendary. The Paddy was still on its ridiculous 72-minute schedule from Stranraer Harbour to Girvan, but frequent late starts from Stranraer Harbour gave ample opportunity for time recovery. I never got the times of that famous night when Mitchell was alleged to have made up no less than 31 minutes between Stranraer and Glasgow. The following log appears to be the fastest of Mitchell's runs of which I have a record. Curiously enough, he had not his own No 1179 that night, but No 912, lately transferred from Ardrossan.

49

Train: 9.27pm	*Engine No*: 912	
Date: 22 December 1930	*Load*: 121 tons	

Stranraer Harbour	*dep*	10.12pm	45 minutes late
Dunragit		10.22pm	
New Luce		10.32pm	
Glenwhilly		10.39pm	
Barrhill		10.50pm	
Pinwherry		10.54pm	
Pinmore		11.00pm	
Girvan	*arr*	11.07pm	
	dep	11.10pm	
signals Kilkerran			
Maybole		11.27pm	
Ayr	*arr*	11.37pm	
	dep	11.40pm	
special stops, Troon and Irvine			
severe signal checks,			
Kilwinning and Millikenpark			
Paisley	*arr*	12.29am	
	dep	12.30am	
St Enoch	*arr*	12.40am	25 minutes late

I think that, given a clear road and no special stops, he could *just* have made up the 31 minutes. Oh, those special stops! Any passenger from Ireland, on giving notice at Larne, could have the Paddy stopped to set down at any station between Stranraer and Paisley. This was a great convenience for passengers at that late hour of night, but not much of a help to a driver wanting to get home himself. Sam Mitchell had nine special calls one night! The Paddy always had to take the loop line through Troon Passenger in case a stop was called. Charlie Seivewright was coming off the Troon loop at Barassie one night of a wild storm, and as he curved to the main line No 1180 slowed almost to a stop with the force of the wind. I always thought No 1180 the strongest of the Corkerhill compounds. Fred Hough brought 248 tons from Stranraer on the Paddy one night with No 1180 – 200 tons was their rostered maximum. Given good conditions, the compounds could do astonishing things. Jock Paterson, working back from Stranraer with a 260-ton train of empty coaches, was stopped at New Luce, started away, and went up the bank without any

50

bother, and I never thought that No 913 was a very strong engine. Norman Peacock was on the return trip of the Sunday Portpatrick train with No 911 and a train of 277 tons. A Girvan fellow who was piloting him with No 14359, a big coal-worrier of a Caley, dropped a plug and had to come off at New Luce. Peacock wanted to divide the train in New Luce station and take it up in two portions. Bob McDonald the guard, a Girvan man, said, 'Oh go on. Try it. It's a fine night. If we stick and have to half them, we'll always be nearer the top.' So Peacock tried it and got up, though McDonald told me that he was twice at the open door with the detonators in his hand, sure that they were stuck.

You will see that Corkerhill had received more compounds. The crazy allocation of 1927 was at last put right. In the summer of 1930 the following changes were made:

> Corkerhill to Ardrossan: No 595, 596
> Ardrossan to Corkerhill: No 911, 912
> Ardrossan to Ayr: No 910
> Hurlford to Ayr: No 915, 916.

In the autumn of that year three English compounds, Nos 1080–2 came to Corkerhill. They were right-hand drive, and when they came had no side doors. Men remarked on their quietness in running without the rattle of side doors. These were very good engines, No 1081 in particular. She was double-shifted with two excellent men, Davie Kirkpatrick and Jimmy McGee, who did fine work until common-user set in.

1930 was the year in which the Big Four took on an extra job, and to my joy Bob Brown came back into the fold. He was given No 912 and managed to keep her for a long time, despite common-user.

That, too, was the year the regular Leeds turns started, and the Big Four, now the Big Five, had to learn another mountain road. It really began back in 1928, when at the England v Scotland football international of that year, four specials were put on from old G&SW territory, to go to London via Leeds, and four compounds, two from Corkerhill and two from Hurlford, were scheduled to haul them as far as Leeds, with conductors from Carlisle. Bob Brown and Mornie Gibson, with No 914, had a special from St Enoch direct over the Barrhead road. Jock Paterson and Willie McCardle with No 913 started from Paisley and took an unusual route via Beith North, Irvine and Springside. John McCrae of Hurlford, with fireman Milroy and No 916 ran the special from Ayr, while Sanny Peden and fireman Craig with No 915 took the one from Kilmarnock. All were piloted to New Cumnock on the up journey, but the Corkerhill crews had no assistance thereafter. They got on very well and were very pleased with themselves.

That was the start. Thereafter at various times the Scottish compounds worked down to England on such excursion work. At Paisley holidays of 1930, Adam Craven with No 914 and a St Enoch class 2P piloting throughout, took a Blackpool excursion of 426 tons. The Scottish enginemen booked off at Preston, the engines being taken to Southport. There was a spot of bother on the return journey, for No 914 had been very lightly coaled, and they had to be careful. However, leaving Preston 17 minutes late, they were on time at New Cumnock and all was under control. Some of those trips were routed over the Caley on the return journey. On one occasion, Jock Paterson reached Law Junction (just south of Wishaw on the Caley main line) to find unfamiliar signals off for him. 'Whaur's this we're gaun?' he demanded. 'We're pitten ye the North road,' the signalman explained. 'But I've never been ower the North road,' says Paterson. 'Ah go on,' replies the signalman, 'it's no' far, an' they'll pit ye back doon at Wishaw Central.' So Jock went on, and managed it. 'Ye've tae watch,' he told me, 'yon's a gey steep bit yonder at Shieldmuir.' It is in fact 1 in 50.

In the summer of 1930 the Big Five were put to learn the Leeds road. Each had a spell, travelling on footplates, and many were the tales of their experiences. One day at Carlisle Sam Mitchell boarded a Claughton to travel to Leeds. It was an eye-opener. Said Mitchell, 'Never in my long experience on the footplate have I ever seen a fireman shovel coal like yon. From when we left

Above: LMS No 14374, Manson 18 class 4-4-0 ex G&SW 157/346.
Real Photographs Co Ltd

Below: Holehouse Junction. Ayr line to left, Rankinston line to right. This
was simply an exchange platform with no external access.
W. A. Camwell

Above: LMS No 14247, Manson 240 class 4-4-0 ex G&SW 241/380.
D. L. Smith collection

Below: Portpatrick station with a train for Stranraer headed by an LMS 2P
4-4-0.
W. Tennant

Carlisle till we turned Ais Gill he only laid the shovel down once, and then he started heavin' lumps.' This was no great exaggeration. Arthur Followes of Durran Hill told me of one night he had a Claughton and a coal inspector was taking records. From Carlisle to Ais Gill they put in 422 shovelfuls, from Carlisle to Leeds 626.

The winter workings of 1930 saw the Big Five with a rostered turn to Leeds. It was only at weekends, but was no sinecure, and began at the start of winter weather and darkness. On the Saturday evening, they took the 5.30pm from St Enoch, came off at Carlisle at 8.15pm, and went forward on the lighter train which came off the Waverley, due Leeds at 11.36pm. On the Monday morning they got the night sleeper that had come from St Pancras, left at 2.12am and worked right through to Glasgow, arriving 7.32am.

With engines in good order these jobs were well within their power, but already the chill blast of economy was being felt, and there were difficulties. Here is one of my notes of an early experience of Bob Brown (11–13 October 1930). Archie Brown (no relation) was firing: 'Engine 912. 5.30pm to Leeds. 247 tons ex-St Enoch, 1 extra from Dumfries. 198 tons from Carlisle. Conductor from there. Monday morning on duty 12.40. Engine not coaled. Put on eleven buckets and needed it. Very big lumps and constant breaking. Left 3 late, 282 tons to Carlisle, 309 tons from there. No assistance. Into St Enoch on time though stopped outside. Fire badly clinkered.'

On 28 December 1930, Sam Mitchell was on the Leeds, with No 1179 and Harry McGeorge firing. They had over their load and were piloted to New Cumnock. It was a wild night of storm. They got only to Barrhead and were held up there. In front of them was a Caley man with a long train of empties for Glengarnock. He had a Corkerhill conductor. They were to shunt for the 5.30pm at Neilston; in the dark they drew up too far, went over a set of catch-points, and in setting back, derailed. So the 5.30pm sat at Barrhead for an hour and a half till they got him back on the rails. Of course when they got to Carlisle their usual light train from Edinburgh was long since gone; they had to go on, with no interval, with their heavy Glasgow train. They got a Carlisle man on as conductor.

Still it raged and blew as they hammered their way up the valley. Harry was getting into difficulties. The storm, the long delay, and the heavy train had eaten into his coal supply, and there had been no time at Carlisle to get some forward. By Kirkby Stephen the coal was beyond his reach. Now compound tenders had no front doors; you had to climb over a fairly high bulkhead, not a nice job in the dark on a strange road where you did not know the over-bridges. Sam Mitchell was sitting on the fireman's side. Harry told him what was wrong. 'Better tell the conductor,' says Sam. Harry did so, and got a snappy answer. 'What's he sayin'?' asked Mitchell. 'He says I'm to get into the tender and get some forrit,' replied Harry. Sam bounced up. 'There's no fireman of mine going up into that tender tonight!' he shouted. The conductor nearly blew up! 'Oh, this has never happened to me before!' he wailed. 'Weel,' says Mitchell, 'it has happened tae ye *noo*. What are ye goin' tae dae aboot it?' He did not know. 'Get a grip o' yoursel',' says Mitchell, 'you're near the top. Take it easy across tae Bleamoor, then she'll run doon the hill. Ye'll just need to go in at Hellifield and get a bucket o'coal.' So on they went, and down the hill amid the lamentations of the conductor, but good old No 1179 did not fail. They were just past Settle Junction when a tender axlebox blazed up, so they had to come off at Hellifield for a hot box, and nobody knew they were short of coal!

But life was not all Corkerhill compounds and expeditions to England. Work was going on very briskly in old G&SW country, where the LMS class 2P 4–4–0s were going from strength to strength. Some more came up from England about the end of 1930: Nos 606/7 went to Girvan, Nos 608/9 to Ardrossan and Nos 610/11 to Princes Pier. These were second-hand off the Midland, but in August 1931 another fifteen came, brand-new out of Crewe. Corkerhill got Nos 636/40, Dumfries Nos 641/2, Girvan Nos 643/4, Stranraer Nos 645/6, Ayr Nos 647/8, and St Enoch Nos 649/50.

There were some great engines in that contingent. No 644 at Girvan was marvellous. In one of their dafter diagrams, the LMS rostered the Girvan engine to work the 12.30pm ex-St Enoch on Saturdays. This, the Stranraer train, was liable to load up to 13 coaches on Saturday, including a Pullman diner, and to get that lot 'over the Union', as the men called the 1 in 100 up to Cumberland Street from the Clyde bridge, was asking a fair amount of a class 2P, but the Girvan men did it. I never heard of one sticking. Sam McKnight had 387 tons one Saturday with No 644. Allowed 41 minutes for the 33.7 miles from Paisley to Ayr, he took 42 minutes 20 seconds. He was quite apologetic about it. 'I had to work her pretty hard,' he said. I have no doubt about that.

No 647 of Ayr was my favourite. She was a lovely wee engine and gave me my first 75mph on the Glasgow road. High speeds were not very common on the Glasgow road of 1934. Up to that time I had never got over 70mph with any class, G&SW or LMS, yet this class 2P lilted up to 75mph apparently without effort. I will always remember one evening when I went up with her to Muirkirk. For some reason those Ayr–Muirkirk trains were very hard booked. The distance is $27\frac{3}{4}$ miles, with a vertical rise of 825ft, and a 62 minute booking. This included ten stops, at little platforms which barely accommodated the three bogie coaches. We arrived in Cumnock A&C two minutes before time, and thought we were doing rather well. It was winter time, and falling dusk; as we went up from Cronberry to Muirkirk the big snow wreaths were looming up ghost-like in the cuttings.

The Girvan class 2Ps got quite a lot to do. There had been big changes in the Stranraer service. In the summer of 1931, the new steamer *Princess Margaret* was placed on the Larne run. The vessel had very fine sleeping accommodation. A new train left Glasgow at 8.00pm, arriving Stranraer 10.57pm. Passengers could then go aboard and have a full night's sleep. To balance the coach workings another new train, a semi-fast, was put on at 7.20pm from Stranraer. Then the 5.10pm from Glasgow worked through to Stranraer instead of the 4.10pm. The Big Five worked the 5.10pm to Girvan and returned on the 7.20pm ex-Stranraer. The Girvan men, with their class 2Ps, took the 5.10pm onto Stranraer and brought the Paddy back to Girvan. The Corkerhill 2P link ran the 8.00pm to Girvan, returning with the Paddy. Stranraer men brought the 7.20pm to Girvan and returned with the 8.00pm. Loads were not heavy as yet, but it was interesting to see how the class 2Ps were getting the lion's share of the work. At Corkerhill, there was still a fair amount of 'one-man-one-engine'. Johnnie Caven got No 636, Cockle Joe Johnstone No 637, Bob Balmer No 638 and Trencher Scott No 639. I do not remember who had No 640.

Balmer was always funny about a transfer to another engine. The engine he had previously was endowed with all possible virtue. His fresh acquisition was condemned utterly. Balmer had been running No 14673 (ex-512 ex-128), the Manson superheater 4–6–0, and had been doing good work. Now he was given this unknown, No 638. One day at Corkerhill he was standing at the front of No 638 when the foreman passed by. Balmer called him over. He pointed to the front buffer. 'Dae ye see that buffer?' asked Balmer. 'Aye,' replied the foreman, a bit mystified. 'Come on then,' said Balmer, and he walked the foreman down to the rear of the tender. 'Dae ye see *that* buffer?' 'Aye.' 'Then,' said Balmer, 'between the twae o' them there's nothing but a damt heap o' scrap!' A fortnight later he was boasting of the prowess of No 638, and was ready to back her against all comers!

Balmer and I became great pals. I learned his ways, and not to bother him unduly on mornings when his asthma was bad. He was a great runner, game for anything. I came with him on the Paddy one night. No 638 was in great form, and as we raced through Maybole station in 16 minutes 10 seconds from Girvan, I was all set for a record time to Ayr. Then to my great surprise Balmer shut his regulator. We were going down past Maybole Junction when I crossed over and asked diffidently if there was a permanent way slack. 'No,' said Balmer, 'Nae pw. Last nicht she very nearly ran tae Ayr withoot steam. She's gaun tae dae it the nicht!' This was a proposition. All right at the first; we could roll down to the Doon viaduct at Cassillis, but then came a good two miles of upgrade to Dalrymple Junction, with a mile of 1 in 90 included, before the final descent to Ayr. The locomotive would never do it. We went down fast to the Doon all right. Even by Dalrymple station we were still doing well. Then on the 1 in 90 we began to flag. Down the speed went, down, down, and down went my confidence accordingly. It was a very dark night. I remember the fireman and I leaning over the side trying to get a sight of that precious white board with the word *level* on it. I remember turning and calling 'She'll never do it, Bob!' Balmer sat immovable on top of the reverser, his arms folded across his chest. 'Aye, she'll dae it!' he said. We got to the level and there was the signalbox – and there, of course, was the signalman, standing at the window with his mouth open! He would be due off duty as soon as he got out-of-section for us, and here, he was quite sure, was an engine failure, at 11 o'clock at night! But we rolled slowly past him at about 5mph and then away we went. We were allowed 12 minutes from passing Maybole to arriving in Ayr. We had taken 12 minutes 10 seconds.

That was what the class 2P could do with the by-pass valves. By-pass valves and bogie brakes were all ripped off – too much bother for the fitters – and the engines were never the same. We got another batch up from England later with yet another gadget on them, vacuum pumps. They were removed likewise. That was the batch Nos 661–70. I heard also that there was a bit of a scare with those engines. They had come to Scotland and were in traffic when someone in the LMS Northern Division offices at 302 Buchanan Street raised the alarm that they had never been cut down to the Scottish loading gauge, so they went very quickly to the shops. Nos 661–5 went to Hurlford, Nos 667/8 to Ardrossan, Nos 669/70 to Corkerhill, No 666 went, I understand, to Stirling, but became rather a wanderer upon the face of the earth. No 670 at Corkerhill got the reputation of a very fast engine, but I never got an opportunity of timing it on any worthwhile job. The final hand-out was a bunch of four new ones out of Crewe, Nos 686–9, with snap-head rivets on the tenders. They all went to Hurlford.

While the LMS passenger engines had been establishing themselves on the old Sou'West, goods engines had been creeping in too. Ayr got 4F 0–6–0s Nos 4182–4 as early as 1926. Sanny Bryden No 2 and Jock Murray got No 4182 and liked her well. They told me that they took 42 empties Ayr Harbour to New Cumnock in 70 minutes, and a load of 55 of goods Dumfries to New Cumnock was no trouble. Also they had left Girvan with a full load of loco coal and passed Pinmore in 23 minutes. Corkerhill did not get any of those class 4Fs until early 1928, when Sanny Wills received No 4321 and, I think, Jimmy Seivewright No 4322, on the 1.00am. They reported them seven minutes faster than the Drummonds Girvan to Pinmore and I have no doubt that coal consumption was greatly reduced.

It did not always work out so well, though. On 20 October 1930 the 1.00am College–Stranraer goods had a superheater class 4F, and Control had a nice little scheme lined up. Ayr shed was instructed that the customary pilot engine should be another class 4F. At Girvan the train engine was to go on to Stranraer with full single-engine load, while the pilot came off, turned, and took 55 empties from Girvan to Mossblown. It was the time of the autumn leaf-fall, and in Glendoune cutting, deep in the woods, the rails might as well have been soft-soaped. They got up into the cutting and stuck, spinning hopelessly. They had to divide the train, and as Pinmore was by then switched-out for most of the time, the first portion had to be taken to Pinwherry, seven miles on, before returning for the remainder. The pilot meantime had started up through the woods in the Ayr direction. They took 30 minutes to pass Killochan, $2\frac{1}{2}$ miles, then stuck altogether above Dailly, set back to there, shunted their train, and beetled back to Girvan with the tank dry! I do not suppose Control had ever heard of the leaf-fall, but they should have been warned. Only five days before the 1.00am episode, the great Sam Mitchell had been brought to his knees – I believe, the only time that that happened to him.

Before I tell you this story you must know the characteristics of the two men principally involved, drivers Sam Mitchell of

Corkerhill and Sam McKnight of Girvan. Both were highly competent enginemen. Both knew that this was so, but Mitchell regarded all Girvan men as only one jump off the plough-boy, and lost no opportunity of taking them down. Both Mitchell and McKnight were well-educated men with a fine command of correct English, and Mitchell had a blisteringly sarcastic tongue. To hear those two conducting a conversation in polite phrasing, was a delight – McKnight infinitely watchful, weighing his words, Mitchell with the eye of an eagle, ready to pounce. They reminded me of two dogs, stalking round one another, with their hair bristling!

On 15 October 1930, Mitchell was on the 4.10pm through to Stranraer with No 1179. Harry McGeorge was firing. It was a beast of a night, stormy and wet, rain changing to sleet as the train went up the hill. They got to Girvan and the two rear coaches were detached for Turnberry, leaving 196 tons to go on south. The man with the Turnberry coaches gave them a push the length of the platform, then departed, and the van was scarcely off the platform end when No 1179 went into a furious slip and stuck. Most drivers would then have set back into the station and waited for assistance, but not Mitchell. He banged at it and managed to get away, but only went to the advance signal and stuck again. He got away and stuck twice up in Glendoune, off again by some miracle, only to stick finally up at the waterworks. Harry McGeorge had to take the tablet and walk back $2\frac{1}{2}$ miles in the dark.

Harry got down eventually, but Girvan could not help him. He must wait until the local from Ayr via Turnberry came in, which arrived with Manson 4–4–0 No 14161 (ex-414 ex-73) with Driver Sam McKnight and Fireman Billy Rae. They were informed that they had to go up and bank Mitchell. McKnight was not at all pleased, for he was an elder in the parish church, and there was a Kirk Session meeting that night. However, he hurried up, rounded his train, stowed it in the siding, got Harry and his tablet aboard, and off to the rescue.

By that time regular assistance in rear had been sanctioned for

61

Glendoune bank. The banking engine would get a banking key from Girvan No 3 box, would not couple to the train, and at milepost $3\frac{3}{4}$, about a quarter-mile from the summit, would drop off and return to Girvan. But it was laid down that if an engine had to go to *assist* a train stuck in the section, then it must have the tablet belonging to that train, must couple to its rear, and go through the section to its first stop at Pinmore. So they went up, found the rear of the train, Billy Rae got down to couple, and Harry went off with his tablet, McKnight telling him that he would give two crows when he was ready. Billy Rae climbed up again, McKnight gave two crows, Mitchell gave two in answer and off they went ... for about a coach length, and stopped. McKnight glanced up; the vacuum needle was at zero! Billy Rae clapped his hand to his mouth. 'Oh,' he said, 'I've coupled the bags and forgot the coupling!'

It may sound funny but it's easier done than you'd think. Out in the dark with the sleet trickling down your neck, groping under a rear gangway for a stiff vacuum hose, you get set on the job of coupling that to the tall swan-neck on the engine, and forget the primary job of the coupling itself. McKnight and Rae got down to see what damage had been done. The engine was sitting about 10ft from the rear of the train. They examined the bag on the engine, which did not appear to be damaged. They replaced it on its plug. Then they groped for the van bag. It seemed to be all right; they put it on its plug.

All this time Mitchell had not tumbled to the situation at the rear. He was roaring, bashing and slipping, and just as they replaced the van bag he thought that he would try in reverse! McKnight and Rae were still down on the ground when back he came − Billy slipped out from between with not an inch to spare. Bang they went into No 14161, which rolled off down the 1 in 54! There was a situation, the old Manson moving off into the dark, with two desperate men in pursuit. McKnight was middle-aged, with some corresponding spread; he just managed to touch a buffer with the tips of his fingers. Wee Billy was like a whippet; running furiously, he got a hold of the side step, wriggled on to it, climbed up, and along to the cab and stopped her. McKnight met up. 'Come on,' he said, 'never mind coupling or anything.' He buffered up to the rear, and away with them. Up they went right to the top, then they had to keep steaming down through the tunnel in case they lost the train. Finally they pulled up in Pinmore station about six feet from the van. The guard had to see to parcels, then he came and looked. 'Oh, you're tied off,' he said, 'Cheer-o, boys!' and off they went.

Then 14161's crew tried to raise vacuum and could not do so. The bag *had* been damaged. They took it off, went over into the wood, got a bit of stick and made a plug. When they got home, they just put in the repairs book, 'Front bag to renew' and no one ever queried it.

Meantime the 4.10pm pursued its interrupted journey. Due at Stranraer at 7.35pm, they arrived at 9.05pm. They got to the sheds at 9.12pm, turned, took two buckets of coal and six pails of sand, and whistled out at 9.25pm. I expect they would have to take their train to the Harbour, so did well to get away at 9.51pm, 24 minutes late. They had special stops at Barrhill and Pinwherry and took water at Girvan, arriving 19 minutes late in Ayr at 11.27pm.

Sam McKnight told me this story the following week, but extracted from me a solemn promise that never,,must I ever let Sam Mitchell know what went on at the rear of his train that night. I never did so, but as all four participants have now passed on, I can put it in print for the first time.

5

Common User

It must not be thought that all additions to the stock of the G&SW section were new or near-new superheater engines. 1928 saw the inevitable influx of Caledonian cast-offs, bestowed charitably upon its poor relation. In the spring of 1928, No 14340 (CR 890) came to Girvan. For a time it worked on the Girvan–Glasgow job and did quite well, but ran up a big-end very badly. The cab arrangements rather shocked me. They were the proverbial plumber's nightmare. Then Stranraer got three Caleys, Nos 14333/4/59. They looked small compared with the LMS class 2Ps, but we got to know that their fame, established long ago when they came out as members of the Dunalastair family, had not entirely departed. One day in the summer of 1931, No 14333 left Girvan with a train of 188 tons and topped the summit at milepost 4 in 15 minutes 10 seconds. I heard the next week, purely by chance, that the officiating expert on this occasion had been William McDowall, whose nickname was 'Coffee'. As Stranraer ignores the 'Mc', the rendering in the vernacular was 'Coffee Doal'. Coffee had been boasting of his exploit in the bothy at Stranraer. 'Aye,' he said, 'fifteen meenits tae the tunnel. The water wasna in sicht till we were awa' doon by the Keeper's.' That would be at least six minutes after they came over the top.

Then there was the exploit of No 14334 at the Glasgow Fair period of 1933. Sanny McCloy was driving and Davie Morrison firing. They were given a train of empty coaches, 230 tons, to take to Glasgow. No assistance was available. They went on alone and ran Midday Paddy time to Pinmore. There they were looped for a long time and a tube began to leak. It got worse and worse, and by Maybole the brakes were rubbing as the pressure dropped.

Finally they ground to a stand at Ayr No 2 home signal. Morrison went to the box to summon assistance. When he got back McCloy was throwing the fire out; the water was out of sight even with both injectors on! To go on to Glasgow they were given a Whitelegg 4–4–0 rebuild. It had no firedoor.

In 1928 the Stranraer men got back their old job on the Port Road Paddy (the Stranraer boat train to Carlisle and the south over the Portpatrick & Wigtownshire Joint line via Newton Stewart and Castle Douglas). They left Stranraer at 9.42pm, into Carlisle at 12.52am, leaving at 2.33am, into Stranraer at 5.10am. For this they were given two Pickersgill 4–4–0 superheaters, Nos 14492/3. Though hardly as steep as the Girvan Road, the Port Road was hard going, and loads could be heavy. I have a note of an occasion on 16 September 1932, when the 9.42pm was loaded thus: postal sorting carriage, four for Newcastle, a van and a third for Carlisle, and a London portion consisting of two composite sleepers, one first sleeper and a van, 402 tons in all. As the Pickersgills were only class 3P and rated for a maximum load of 225 tons, piloting was frequent.

In December 1931, Jimmy Shankland came off the Paddy job by reason of advancing years and Andrew McKenzie got his place. Andrew's first week on the Paddy was not devoid of incident. It was a week of wild storm. They coaled the Paddy engine at Kingmoor, and the first night they required eleven buckets, which I understand was not unusual. The next night they were very late, there was no time to coal, so they were given a decrepit Caley for the return journey. Its mouthpiece was all choked up in past efforts to make it steam, and it was throwing fire like a small volcano. However, they got to Stranraer without mishap, and back that following night as far as Gretna. There they got a signal stop, and in lifting away again they set the rear gangway of the postal on fire. They stopped in the section with the gangway blazing. The postal men got their mail bags out on to the line side at the double, while fireman John Brown ran back and forward over the roof of the postal with buckets of water. They got the fire out without great damage. At Kingmoor they were given back their own locomotive. The next night they blew a tube and had to get No 645 to finish the week.

The Stranraer men liked the Pickersgills, though. Nos 14507/8 came to Stranraer as well. Andrew McCreadie told me that he fired for two years to Willie Lithgow on No 14507 and got on well. The Pickersgills were pretty sure-footed, though Lithgow stuck on the Neck one frosty morning on the early train out of Stranraer with No 14492. He was heavy-laden that morning, with additions of a sleeper and a composite for a party going to Barrhill, and an empty diner off the 8.00pm of the night before.

There were always two down Paddies on the Port Road. The first, at 2.33am out of Carlisle, took the London coaches, including the Euston–Turnberry sleeper. The second waited for the down West Coast Postal and got the Stranraer sorting carriage off it. It also conveyed the through coach from Newcastle. This second Paddy left at 3.13am, and as far as Dumfries was combined with the Ayr train (it also had a sorting carriage). A St Enoch class 2P worked the 3.13am to Dumfries and took on the Ayr portion; a Dumfries class 2P worked the Stranraer.

On the Girvan–Stranraer section the years 1932/3 were relatively peaceful. The men were well content with their class 2Ps; they steamed well, were speedy and could climb hills. Moreover, they were not addicted to slipping. Derby had laid down a top load for them, 135 tons in each direction south of Girvan, but this was a ridiculous figure. On the Paddy, Geordie Thomson with No 644 took 181 tons from Stranraer Harbour to Girvan in 63 minutes 25 seconds; Tom Prestly with No 643 took 180 tons over the same course in 63 minutes 20 seconds. Sam McKnight had No 607 on the Midday Paddy with 183 tons, and took the scheduled 67 minutes with the Dunragit stop and a permanent way slack at New Luce viaduct, of all places. They were strange engines in some ways. Let them be doing, say, 30mph on a long bank with an even gradient, and they would keep it up, but one could not expect them to slow down to 20mph, maybe for a permanent way slack and then get up to 30mph again.

Still, they were very good, but I think the traffic authorities must have seen the figure of 135 tons in the load book, and were shocked thereby. This would not do — they must have more power. Compounds, power class 4, had been on before, so put them on again. The diagrams, however, did not allow the previous working, so they took a short cut. The 5.10pm would be worked by the Big Five and their compounds as far as Girvan, where they would be remanned by Girvan men for the run to Stranraer and back! The howl that went up from the Big Five might have been heard in Euston! To give their precious compounds to be handled by those ignorant savages was too much. Already quarrelling among themselves, internal strife was far surpassed by the venom directed at the Girvan men. The 5.10pm would come into Girvan, the Corkerhill men would grab their kit and march off without a word or a look at their hated supplanters! Then they had the humiliation of walking down to the sheds and looking for the other engine with which they would run the 7.13pm ex-Stranraer back to Glasgow. When new diagrams came out, compounds worked through to Stranraer on all trains.

Then slipping trouble started. Even before the new arrangement began there had been some sore upsets caused by compounds slipping on the Stranraer road. The events of 28 July 1933 may have been exceptional, but they served as an awful warning. The Paddy was now leaving Stranraer Harbour at 9.17pm, and booked to run to Girvan in 66 minutes. That night they left 48 minutes late, with thirteen on, 387 tons, passengers packed in the corridors and the vans full. Tom Prestly was on it with No 643, and Sam Bell of Ayr was piloting with No 1182. Just through New Luce, No 1182 began slipping. Sam Bell could not get her out of compound working and they stuck. They divided the train and took it up in two portions to Glenwhilly. At Girvan Prestly and No 643 came off, and Adam Craven with No 914 came on. Orders awaited them: 'Put an extra coach on rear.' The gymnastics involved in this operation extended the stop to 33 minutes. At Ayr Sam Bell and No 1182 came off and a van was attached, again at the rear. They were lucky, at that time of morning, to find a St Enoch engine working home, so it coupled on in front. They had three special stops, Glengarnock, Johnstone and Elderslie. Then at Paisley there was consternation; an engine was waiting to take the three rear coaches to Dundee, and these had been shut in by the two vehicles attached. So those had to be sorted out, an exercise for which Paisley Gilmour Street was not well arranged. They got to St Enoch at 2.50am, 170 minutes late, and found mails for Ayr still reposing in the Glasgow van!

After a circus like that, one would have thought that a searching inquiry would have been made, but evidently not. London probably never heard of those things, and in Scotland, if the Caley territory was all right, nothing else mattered. From 1930 to 1936, I have a note of 28 occasions on which a passenger train stuck in the section. My list may not be a complete one. Seventeen of those failures took place on Glendoune bank, ten were on New Luce bank, usually at the Swan's Neck, and one was on the climb out of Portpatrick. On Glendoune, in six instances the train was able to restart, in eight the fireman walked back to Girvan and got assistance, and in three the train was divided. In all ten on New Luce bank the train had to be divided, and the same procedure followed at Portpatrick. Engines involved in those incidents comprised one G&SW Drummond 4–4–0, three Caley 4–4–0s, and 24 LMS compounds.

It may be that the authorities could not understand our difficulties, for on other sections the compounds were doing so well. All of the Big Five, on the 1.50pm (now 2.00pm) were taking trains of 400 tons and more over Beattock in grand style. Sam Mitchell surpassed himself on a day when the 2.00pm was divided into Glasgow and Edinburgh portions. With No 1179, he took 394 tons unassisted from Glasgow to Carlisle non-stop. Returning on the 6.34pm, he had 367 tons and passed New Cumnock in 47 minutes from Dumfries. Bob Brown did this stretch in the scheduled 45 minutes, with No 912 and 366 tons. Jock Paterson, with No 913 and 350 tons, took 45 minutes 10 seconds. This run was timed by Mr O. S. Nock, who states that on it he recorded speeds which gave him the highest figure for equivalent drawbar horsepower which he ever had from a compound. Big Jock was a hard hitter, but he was a grand man for looking after an engine. I wish I knew who fired on this occasion. From contemporary notes, it may have been Hughie Sloan, a nice lad and a good fireman.

The compounds were grand for lines like those, where the slipping probably took place only at starting. On the grades and curves of the Stranraer road, slipping was liable to start in all places the least slippery, and could result in a dead stand right away. The compounds had plenty of power but not enough adhesion. What was needed for the Stranraer road was a 4–6–0, and Stranraer table could not turn a 4–6–0.

But there *was* a way out, if those at the top would see it. For some years the Hughes 2–6–0s had been working in Scotland. The first we saw in the Ayr district came in on the Perth goods. I have a note of Nos 13183/4, and 13205–9. They sojourned in Ayr for about 12 hours, so Ayr got permission to employ them on a passenger turn to Glasgow. It was 1935 before I was able to make a trip on this train, the 11.15am from Ayr. No 2909 (by then renumbered out of the 13xxx series) was on it, with 170 tons and the redoubtable Poker Ross driving. The only real 'run' on that mild-mannered train was the 15.9 miles Kilwinning to Johnstone. On that, a compound might just have reached 60mph, maybe not, but this small-wheeled engine got right up to 72mph and held that, without fuss or fireworks. We passed Millikenpark, 14.5 miles, in 15 minutes 20 seconds, then had a signal check. That was an eye-opener. Here was the answer to Stranraer road problems. Simply station as many 2–6–0s at Stranraer as would cover the workings to Girvan and Dumfries. Compounds and class 2Ps could work successfully beyond those points, and Stranraer could turn a 2–6–0.

There was little haste to do anything for the Stranraer district. In the summer of 1935 we heard that Stranraer men had got a 2–6–0 for the Paddy job. It was a Kingmoor engine, changed at Carlisle when necessary. The Pickersgills had been giving serious trouble with the heating of the coupled wheel axleboxes. There was still a fair Caley influence on the Port Road. Kingmoor, a Caley shed, could not let the side down. We heard that the men liked those 2–6–0s. By 1936, the Kingmoor 2–6–0s were working the 11.41am Stranraer to Glasgow and the 3.50pm boat train back, in the interval of their time at Stranraer.

I timed several of those trains that summer. Hill-climbing was excellent and there was no slipping. There was plenty of speed where it was required. The G&SW men had a great respect for those engines. They always called them 'Moguls'. The cheap sneer of the term 'Crab' by which they were known on other parts was never heard on the Sou'-West.

All would have been very well but the LMS, the right hand never knowing what the left was doing, now upset all good plans. They decreed that engine-changing between Glasgow and Stranraer must be abolished, and they accelerated many of the Ayr–Glasgow trains by very considerable amounts. Trains which had kept time with a maximum speed of 60mph had now to do 70mph and plenty of it. So, of course, if the Stranraer road was to be worked by Moguls, those must work also to the new schedules between Ayr and Glasgow. The Moguls could do those speeds, but it was a different thing doing 72mph by an odd time and doing it mile after mile for days on end.

The 12.30pm ex-St Enoch was a through working, with an Ayr Mogul, remanned at Ayr. Rumours of those high speeds with those engines must have travelled down south, for a Crewe inspector came up and travelled on the 12.30pm engine, with the famous Anthony Ross. By the time they were approaching Dalry the coals were rolling out of the side doors and the inspector was shouting 'Ease her off! Ease her off!' 'Ease nothing,' says Ross, 'I'm two minutes down already.' His spell in Scotland did not do the inspector's nerves any good.

Certainly they did not put them on the two non-stop trains, the 8.27am ex-Ayr and the 5.10pm ex-St Enoch. Those were allowed 45 minutes for the 41.4 miles, a harder booking than it looks. Both were well-patronised trains, loading to about 290 tons. The 8.27am got VIP treatment. Each morning a class 5X, later known

Above: LMS No 14674, Manson superheater 4-6-0 ex G&SW 129/513 at Glasgow (St Enoch) in August 1929.
D. L. Smith collection

Below: LMS No 14517, P. Drummond 4-4-0 ex G&SW 138/326.
D. L. Smith collection

Above: Pinwherry station, looking south.
H. D. Bowtell

Below: LMS No 14509, four-cylinder 4-4-0 ex G&SW 11/394, named *Lord Glenarthur*.
Real Photographs Co Ltd

as a Jubilee, from Patricroft shed, worked up to Glasgow on a newspaper express from Manchester. With one of those engines, a Polmadie man ran a parcels train to Ayr, and went back with the 8.27am. Their running was another eye-opener to me. The engines seemed to be very well kept, and the Polmadie men seemed well accustomed to fast work. I had some great running behind those men – Willie Bell, George Melville, Willie Melville, Bob Ross, Bob Alcorn, George Palmer, James Brown, Andrew Carnie and others.

Ayr shed had the job on Saturday mornings, and how they let it down! They had no class 5X locomotives. They used to turn out their poorest compound, No 1182, and had a genius for arranging things so that the driver was someone spare, on for holiday relief, or such excuse. These men had no experience of running a train as hard as this, and little to do it with anyway.

The 5.10pm was let down similarly. It was given to a link of Corkerhill men, about the third link I should imagine, with compounds. Now the Corkerhill compounds of 1936 were certainly not the compounds of 1927/8. It was common-user manning now, with all its evils, in addition to which they were overhauled at Polmadie. Polmadie might be expert at maintaining a Caley, but they could not set compounds' valves. The men in the link were not a brilliant lot, and like the Ayr men, had had no experience of running such as was necessary on this train. So I had a series of poor runs, with some maddening delays thrown in for good measure. Imagine being stopped at Arkleston for an intermediate tail-lamp! Then one night there was a 'foreign' compound, No 1066, but the young hand on it could not get it to start. He tried to reverse, but the train was hard in to the buffers. They worked away for about fifteen minutes until the shunting pilot gave them a pull out! Then another night they had a gas tank going down to Portpatrick, and some clown stuck it on the front of the 5.10pm. It was as old as the hills and by Irvine two axleboxes were blazing. They had a 'stop and examine' at Monkton, and then crawled into Ayr 15 minutes late.

One Ayr man did put up a show one Saturday morning, 11 July

1936, my old friend Jimmy Robson No 2, with Sam Brown firing. They were put on this 8.27am job, and were not even given a compound, but a Pickersgill 4–4–0, No 14474, which had just come to Ayr. They had a load of 284 tons, passed Troon Goods in their allotted time of eight minutes, passed Beith North in $24\frac{1}{2}$ minutes, and were stopped by signals on Clyde Bridge at 9.10am, and arrived in St Enoch on time at 9.12am.

Jimmy Robson was the man who fired to the Auld Juck that night in 1905 when they did the record run from Stranraer Harbour to Ayr in 76 minutes. Jimmy was a grand hand. I remember 29 October 1938 when I was on the 1.52pm Ayr to Glasgow (11.41am ex-Stranraer), Jimmy Robson and Hughie Gordon with No 910 and $368\frac{1}{2}$ tons – eleven and the Pullman diner. We left Paisley along the four track section right on the heels of a Caley 18in 0–6–0 on an up Gourock with eight on, about 230 tons. By Greenlaw he was well ahead, then we began to pull up on him. By Hillington West we were alongside and gaining, coach by coach. The row was terrific. We were just past Hillington East when down came the black smoke and on went our brakes, and we came down to 10mph past Cardonald Station box. At St Enoch, I commiserated with Robson over his unfortunate signal check. 'The pity of it,' said Robson, 'was that it was clear for me, but the Caley man blinded it with his smoke, and I couldn't take a chance.' No 910 was a splendid engine, then it went for an overhaul to Polmadie, and lost all its sparkle.

I went down to Stranraer one Saturday on No 910, with Anthony Ross and Jimmy Cairns. We had 166 tons south of Girvan. It was an awful day, raining steadily, and the hill-mist down almost to the sleeper-ends. The tender was down to the coal dust, and with the rain, it was like black porridge. When the LMS compounds were just coming out, I remember a letter in one of the railway publications in which the writer tried to enlighten interested amateurs in the working of those engines. He said that it must always be remembered that a compound had to be fired with the utmost care; a shovelful in the wrong place and down would go the boiler pressure. Jimmy Cairns opened his firedoors wide. Then he plastered up the firehole with this black mud till not a flame showed. He propped himself against the right-hand splasher, shovel in hand, and every time the blast pulled a hole in the 'plaster' he plugged it with another shovelful. Old Tony banged away and she steamed right up to the red mark on the dial!

This reminds me of the time the Corkerhill Big Five had the 1.41am newspaper train added to their roster. This was a train chartered by the Glasgow press to convey the morning papers to Galloway and Northern Ireland. It consisted of one van, and ran non-stop to Dumfries, $82\frac{1}{2}$ miles. Rather than waste a compound on a one-van load, they were given a class 2P, and that week Bob Brown and Mornie Gibson were on it with No 638. They amused themselves by seeing how far they could run before the locomotive needed firing. One morning they were passing Thornhill before it required attention. They determined that the next morning they would go right to Dumfries. At Corkerhill Mornie began piling on coal, more and more, until the coal was nearly on top of the brick arch. They came into St Enoch to pick up their 'train' of one van with not a spark of light showing at the firehole, and there was a train of six vans waiting! What a struggle they had! They just managed to totter over the Shilford; the fire was hardly burned through by New Cumnock.

No 638 was Bob Balmer's engine, but Balmer was not driving it any more. On 6 September 1934, Balmer had swopped for the day with Trencher Scott, so he had Trencher's engine, No 639 and fireman, Willie White, a good lad who had come from Fairlie Pier — an expert at keeping a clean engine. Their job was the 5.35pm ex-St Enoch, a train of many stops, travelling by the Canal line, Beith, Dalry and Montgreenan to Kilmarnock. As usual, soon after leaving St Enoch, they were to be routed through Cumberland Street on the up main, and crossed over at Port Eglinton signal box to the up Canal line. Coming along the down Canal line was the 5.12pm from Paisley West, with No 591 tender-first and a Hurlford crew. The road was set for Balmer, and by signalmen's evidence the Canal down home was against the 5.12pm, but for some reason the Hurlford man ran through it, and the two trains met effectively head-on on the crossing. Balmer and White were killed; the Hurlford fireman died later. Five passengers died, 34 others sustained injury. It was a tragic business.

The Hurlford driver, sole survivor of the footplate crews, had to bear the brunt, first of Colonel Mount's inquiry, then of a trial for culpable homicide. He maintained that the signal was clear for him when he first sighted it; when he was within an engine-length, he looked up again and the signal was at danger. This, of course, implied that the signalman had 'changed the road' after giving him the clear. Colonel Mount, with stop-watch checking, proved that this could not be done in the time. So, by this Ministry of Transport inquiry, the Hurlford driver was at fault. At the subsequent trial, he was acquitted. I shall make no comment; signals can be queer things.

Not long afterwards, on 30 January 1935, another of my Corkerhill friends was in a smash, fortunately without fatal results. The Big Five got a duty on which they took the 2.45am goods from College to Ardrossan, ran light to Largs, and worked one of the morning expresses to St Enoch. Brown was on the goods job that morning with No 912 and Johnnie Jackson firing. There had been a signalling error at Stevenston No 1, and they crashed into the rear of another goods standing on the main line. The collision took place right under the bridge carrying the Caley over the G&SW. This was fortunate, for as No 912 rose on the pile of debris, it hit the bridge and did not tend to fall back on them. No one was seriously hurt, but I always thought that this accident affected Bob Brown's health afterwards; he died some four years later.

Jock Paterson and Bob Brown – that was the original pair from whom developed the Big Four. In Paterson and Brown no one could have found two more contrasting men. Certainly they were efficient enginemen, but there the comparison ended. Paterson was a big, burly man with a stentorian voice if things went wrong; Brown was slight-built and quiet of manner. Paterson was heavy-handed on regulator and brake; Brown's driving and braking were those of an artist. Paterson was a hearty, friendly man, but with little sense of humour; Brown's sense of humour was exquisite.

There was one summer when the Big Four were rostered for both the 5.05pm and the 5.10pm from St Enoch to the Ayrshire coast. The 5.10pm was the prestige train, non-stop to Ayr. The 5.05pm was a summer-only, non-stop to Troon, then to Prestwick and Ayr. It was routed by Canal and North Johnstone, then by the slow line to Dalry No 3, where it joined the main line several minutes after the passing of the 5.10pm, which it followed humbly to Ayr.

On the first night of the summer service Jock Paterson was on the 5.10pm, while Bob Brown had the 5.05pm. Brown went out of St Enoch with No 914 in his usual decorous fashion, but the minute he was over Port Eglinton away he went down the Canal line. The fireman, hard at it and trying to keep his feet, wondered what had come over Brown that night. On they tore round all those curves, through Elderslie on the slow line, down the hole under the main, then bang-crash over Cart Junction and up the hill to Kilbarchan with No 914 roaring like the Bars of Ayr. Over the top, racing down by Castle Semple, 'Ony word o' him?' asked Brown. This was the explanation. No, no sign of the 5.10pm's steam, so down the hill to Lochwinnoch, and up to the long rock cutting and Kilbirnie. Down hill again, and as they raced over the flyover at Brownhill the 5.10pm's white steam was showing beyond Glengarnock. They swung down on to the slow road, past Swinlees, and had just got their tail end round Dalry platform as the 5.10pm was showing in the straight at Brownhill. They got No 2 starter off, raced along to No 3, and drew up at the stop signal. The instant they stopped, Brown grabbed a sweat-rag and shot out along the gangway. So as the 5.10pm swept through, there was Brown, out on the front of No 914, his pipe cocked up at an angle, leisurely polishing his smokebox as if he had been there for a month! And the roars of Big Jock . . .

6
Moguls and 4–6–0s

About 1935 the English job of the Corkerhill top link was changed. The crews still worked up on Friday, but instead of going to Leeds they turned off at Hellifield and terminated at Blackburn. On Saturdays, they worked the 9.15am ex-Manchester (12.46pm off Carlisle) right through to Glasgow. One Friday Jock Paterson had to leave No 913 at Blackburn for some defect, and was given in exchange a class 4F, with which he worked to Carlisle. There he was given No 1145, with a train of 450 tons. No assistance was provided. Allowed 47 minutes to leave Dumfries and pass New Cumnock, he took 51. He was quite huffed about it; he said that if the engine hadn't started priming around Ardoch he would have made a better job.

I had better stop giving the Corkerhill top link any numerical title. With a sixth job added, the old Big Four had lost their identity. The additional member of the party was a rather unexpected one. This goes back in history quite a way.

I was a small boy on holiday in Girvan when I heard of a Bad Man who had come to that peaceful resort. He was an engine-driver, of the name of Reay, and he had come from Carlisle. According to the shocked people of Girvan, he was a socialist, of the red-hot variety, and was spreading dissent among workmates and populace alike. I never saw him, and early in the first world war heard that he had transferred, or been transferred, to the Johnstone Shunt. This was a rather curious G&SW institution. A shunting engine gave round-the-clock service in Johnstone yard. Its two (later three) pairs of men resided in Johnstone, but the engine was supplied from Greenock shed, and was changed every night for the engine of a goods from

Greenock, returning there to coal. Jack Reay put in about 14 years on the Johnstone Shunt, then the LMS, tidying up, moved the Johnstone men to Corkerhill.

Jack Reay claimed his place by seniority, which was on the class 2P link of passenger jobs. With the next shift up, he was in the top link where he was quite an asset! Jack Reay ran the jobs, and ran them very well. He learned the Caley road as well as the Blackburn road and did those in excellent style. 'Woooy, there's nuthin' in the Blackburn road,' he said to me. 'Joost down round the corner from Hellifield.' So after many years I made the acquaintance of this near-anarchist. I found a sturdy, friendly elderly man, of strong character and opinions. I became very friendly with Old Jack, and I may say that he never talked politics to me!

I will always remember an incident associated with Old Jack. It was Glasgow Fair Saturday night of 1937. I was on the Paddy from Stranraer. No 598 with a young Ayr man was piloting No 2880, which was to be re-manned at Girvan. The load was 325 tons. We got to Girvan, and along the platform came Jack Reay and his mate to take over No 2880. 'Go on Jack,' I called to him, 'keep up the good work. That's a good young chap ahead there. He'll give you a good pull.' Old Jack replied, 'It's all right – if they'd keep their —— hands off the brake! They come to me "You take the braking, Jack." Next you know, they pull the —— brake on you!' 'Oh don't you worry, Jack,' I said. 'He's a good lad this. He won't do anything like that.'

We had a fair run to Ayr – nothing exceptional, then . . . I do not know who did what, but we pulled up in Ayr station with the five rear coaches off the platform! When I got forward, there was a row going on – a row of super dimensions. I postponed inquiries and fled! Old Jack may have calmed down in his political opinions, but he had certainly not lost his powers of oratory!

You may ask what had happened to the wild 1.00am College to Stranraer. For a considerable period, nothing adverse did occur. This was largely to the credit of Driver James Halliday, who had transferred from Dumfries to Corkerhill and had come into the

1.00am link. Halliday brought fresh thought to the problem. He viewed the Kilkerran dip as the scene of the worst troubles, so he avoided trouble there by coming to a stop and picking up his couplings gently in the re-start. Soon others were following his example, and for a long time there was little trouble in the Maybole–Girvan section. But of course seniority had to take its course, other men came into the link, and Halliday's teachings began to be forgotten.

On 25 June 1938 there was a bad business at Kilkerran. Matt McCue of Corkerhill was on it with class 4F No 4321, piloted by Bob McMurtrie of Ayr with compound No 910. Somewhere on Crosshill bank they broke away, 10 wagons on the engines and 49 on the van. Douglas was the guard, who they called *Kitchener* because of facial resemblance in younger days. Of course he could not hold 49 wagons, and right in Kilkerran station they overtook the first portion and crashed. This took place alongside the platform, and many wagons were damaged by being derailed and banging against the platform wall. About 300 sleepers were cut. Another breakaway took place on Crosshill bank early in the second world war, on 22 April 1940. I do not know who was involved beyond the fact that the driver of the pilot was the famous Toorie Craig, of Ayr. I saw the signalman's report, which stated that the train went through Kilkerran 'extremely fast, divided 30 and 28, with about eight wagon-lengths between the two portions' – a hair-raising sight! They were luckier on this occasion, for the guard managed to stop the rear portion in Ben's Cut. The first portion ran to Girvan, the engines returning to Kilkerran for the remainder.

Though the grades were steeper and longer south of Girvan, there was an absence of those treacherous changes of grade, and breakaways were very rare. There was one real trap for young players, however – Barrhill station.

From Pinwherry the line climbs to Barrhill for 4 miles 12 chains at an average of 1 in 70. Then alongside Barrhill platform it eases to 1 in 300. The platform is short and at the south end there was a water column, Barrhill being the only watering-point between Girvan and Stranraer. The 1.00am always stopped for water. If, as usual at water columns the train stopped suddenly the first six wagons or so, being on the easier 1 in 300, would buffer up and slacken their couplings. Then after a pause, the rest of the train, still hanging down a 1 in 69, would hang its ponderous weight on the slacked couplings, and bang! I have seen two big engines dragged back 6ft or more with the violent pull they received. And if there was a weakness in the couplings . . .

On 3 November 1927 there was a bad breakaway at Barrhill. Sanny Wills was the Corkerhill driver; I do not know the names of the others. Twenty-nine wagons broke away. They went out through Pinwherry station at high speed, higher, in the opinion of the Pinwherry stationmaster, than that of the train which crashed there in 1928. However, they came to a stand well up the bank towards Pinmore without damage. Another similar incident occurred at Barrhill just before the second world war on 17 May 1939. The Corkerhill driver was one Moncrieff, who had come from St Enoch when that depot closed in 1935. Old Bobby Withers of Girvan was piloting. Somebody stopped suddenly at the column. They got a terrific 'rug', broke a coupling and pulled out a drawbar. The train therefore broke in three parts: four wagons on the engines, 37 on the van, and between them four running free, a wagon of cattle included. The Barrhill signalman nipped round the tail-end of those four and managed to get brakes down before they went over the edge of the 1 in 69. Kitchener, the guard, put on his brake as hard as he could, then jumped off and let the wagons go. They went down through Pinwherry about 60mph and ran to the Stinchar viaduct. The Pinwherry signalman got word that they were coming. He set the down line, then fled across a field, and viewed the proceedings from the safe distance of the main road!

A most destructive breakaway occurred on the Greenock line on 10 April 1936. A train of 37 wagons of cattle left Albert Harbour for Carlisle at 9.00pm, double-headed, the pilot engine being a 2–6–4 tank. They were up about Mearns Street when the pilot slipped violently. In the consequent surge and recoil a coupling broke between the sixth and seventh vehicles. This left 31 on the van, and old Dan Taylor of St John's did his best, but could not hold them. Down they went through the tunnels. At Princes Pier station, No 637 was sitting at Platform 3 with a train made up for Glasgow. Fortunately there were no passengers in it then, and the driver, Archie Davie of Corkerhill, had gone to the guards' room. Tommy Fraser the fireman just jumped clear in time as the runaway crashed into No 637. There was terrible destruction of wagons and beasts. Poor old Dan Taylor was deep in the ruins of his van, and they had a difficult task getting him out. I do not think he was seriously hurt, but he and his rescuers were soaked in blood pouring from the wrecked vehicles. Fifty-one of the cattle were killed or had to be slaughtered.

In G&SW days, the Greenock road had always received great consideration in the respect of its motive power. So it was at this period, in 1936. It could be said to be the one section of the old G&SW which had been provided with engines which were both adequate and suitable. The grand little Manson 4-4-0s were all gone, the class 2Ps had done well with the still rather light trains, but when in December 1933 there came to Princes Pier shed Class 4 2-6-4Ts, Nos 2419-22, a new era in motive power had dawned.

Those were marvellous engines, and the timetable authorities were soon to take advantage of their abilities. For a while in 1938 a working time of eight minutes was allowed for the heavy 5.2-mile climb from the start at Princes Pier to the passing of the box at Upper Port Glasgow. With No 2419 and a load of 113 tons, John Gillies passed Upper Port in 8 minutes 23 seconds, attaining 60mph on the final 1 in 98! I had thought a little Manson doing quite well when, in 1925, she topped Upper Port doing 30mph, although the Manson had a heavier load of 168 tons. Then Jimmy Hyslop, with No 2421, took 12 non-corridor bogie coaches, say 330 tons, from Princes Pier to Crookston, taking 14 minutes to pass Upper Port.

Enginemen on the Glasgow–Stranraer line might well wish that they had been equally well provided for. Although it might appear that with the introduction of the Moguls the problem was solved, it was not, and the reason was to be found in a variety of aspects. First, there was the parsimony with which the Moguls were allotted to this section. Two were given to Corkerhill, and two to Ayr. Those, with the addition of the Mogul from Kingmoor working the first Down Paddy, were supposed to cope with the through Glasgow–Stranraer traffic.

This, of course, could have worked had the Moguls been in good condition, but they varied. There were good and bad – we got to know them. No 2917 was a grand engine; so I believe was No 2918, though I have fewer records of its work. No 2916, on the other hand, was always a poor affair. No 2907–9 formed a good trio. Corkerhill had a contrasting pair. No 2804 was game enough, but it was badly run-down, and became terrible to stand on. No 2880 was a very good one, but unfortunate as regards minor mishaps. Lithgow had No 2880 on the 8.00pm Sunday evening train to Stranraer, and going over the Chirmorie the locomotive broke a front coupled axlebox and a left trailing spring. Lithgow managed to get to Stranraer, however. On 28 April 1938 Sandy McKnight of Girvan had No 2880 on the Paddy. Willie Dummigan was firing. They passed Challoch all right, then just before Donaldson's Crossing there came a loud crack and a sort of sideways shock. Dummigan flew for the handbrake, but McKnight restrained him. 'She's still going,' he said, 'better keep her going and try to get to New Luce than sit down away out here.' So under easy steam they went on, with every now and then a violent punch on the train which even the guard felt five coaches back. At New Luce they found the damage on the left side; the bracket supporting the valve gear had fractured. Stranraer sent them No 646, in good order. At Girvan they handed over to Jimmy McGee who did Girvan–Ayr in 27 minutes and Ayr–St Enoch in 58, with calls at Troon, Irvine and Kilwinning and two permanent way slacks.

Four months later, on 4 September 1938, No 2880 was on the 8.25pm ex-Stranraer Harbour, the last for the summer of the Bangor excursion. They had twelve coaches on, 377 tons, and

Jock Scott of Ayr was piloting with No 1181. They passed Pinwherry and were about a quarter-mile into the section when there was a crack and the same bracket broke again. Ernie McCrindle of Corkerhill, a Girvan-born lad, was on No 2880. The guard wanted to go back to Pinwherry and summon assistance, but the drivers decided that they would have a go. So they started up that bank with a good deal of 1 in 65, No 1181 doing practically all the pulling, only an occasional puff from No 2880. But they got up and through the tunnel and then Scott, much relieved, let the engine go down the hill, to be pulled to a dead stand by Ernie and informed that he, Ernie, valued his life to some extent, even if Scott did not. They crawled down to Girvan, 67 minutes from the point of failure.

Scarcity of Moguls resulted in a reversion to compounds. At busy periods, it was not unusual for the Kingmoor Mogul on the down Paddy, which Stranraer depended upon for the Glasgow job, to have a compound as substitute, Such was the case on 15 August 1936, when James Thomson of Stranraer (always known as 'Sprig') had No 1145 on the Glasgow. Davie Brown was firing. Returning from Glasgow on the 3.50pm, they had a huge train, and Ayr added some, and by incredible blundering Sprig was dispatched unaided with 498 tons! With this he had to climb the $3\frac{1}{4}$-mile bank to Dalrymple Junction, with $\frac{3}{4}$-mile at 1 in 170, a mile at 1 in 88, and at least $1\frac{1}{2}$ miles at 1 in 70. Sprig kept batting at it, and was within three coach-lengths of Dalrymple Junction up home when he stuck. A pilot had been ordered from Ayr shed, but it could not get up to the passenger station in time. No 599 was now brought up, with driver John Brown, lately of Stranraer, and brother of Sprig's fireman. They let him in behind, and he banked them up to Dalrymple Junction, ran round the train via Dalrymple station, and piloted to Stranraer. The load was reduced to twelve from Girvan.

Incidents like this, creditable as the work of the enginemen might be, caused dreadful delays. I should know. I was in the 5.20pm boat train from Stranraer that night. We sat $37\frac{1}{2}$ minutes in the cutting at Barrhill waiting to cross the 3.50pm. Leaving

Stranraer 16½ minutes late, we were 53 minutes late at Girvan. The 3.50pm, when we met her, was 69 minutes late.

The compounds could do wonderful things at times. One Sunday morning the Bangor arrived at Girvan with a train of 293 tons and a Polmadie compound, no pilot. Jock Goudie and Billy Rae re-manned the compound. There was no prospect of assistance; they went on and tried it. It was a lovely sunny morning and the engine never slipped. They took 35 minutes to the tunnel. One slip and they would have been finished.

Those were *good* compounds; they were not all good. Common user methods were killing them. Think of the marvellous condition in which Jock Paterson used to keep No 913. On 10 February 1936 Geordie Thomson of Girvan stuck with her on Glendoune bank with only 170 tons. Here is the report on her condition: 'Showing only 80lb/sq in on low-pressure gauge in simple and 50lb/sq in in compound; steaming wretchedly; hardly any packing in high-pressure piston; blowing off more than 20lb/sq in under pressure.' What could one expect; only into the shed for coal and away with another crew, probably remanned twice before returning. The maintenance staff were not lacking in application, but they were not geared to those conditions.

There was a terrible hold-up on the night of 22 October 1938, with a special excursion returning from the Glasgow Exhibition. They had 13 coaches on, with two compounds, an Ayr driver and a Stranraer driver, and they stuck on Glendoune. With a struggle they got the gangways undone and then discovered that the coupling was nibbed (ie shackled). They tried further back, but could not get one that was free, so had to go forward again. Finally they got going and took the first portion through to Pinwherry, but had to stop at Pinmore as there were passengers for all stations and no one knew where they were in the train. Then they came back, got the second lot, stopped at Pinmore, went on to Pinwherry, stopped there and got the two portions together. Then it was every station, and at the short platforms it took two and sometimes three stops to get all of the train alongside. They were due at Stranraer Harbour station at 2.51am and it was

6.00am before they got in! There were folks in the train for Port Logan and Drummore, and they say that a number of the farm people missed the milking that morning!

I felt sick and sorry over all this, for traffic was booming on this route to Northern Ireland and those wretched happenings were desperately bad publicity. One difficulty was that Pinmore and Glenwhilly were single-platform stations, their loops being for the use of goods trains only. In 1937 a second platform was erected at Glenwhilly, the loop greatly extended, and points laid, which · permitted of a speed of 50mph. This was a help, but it was only one loop. The rest of the miserable short loops remained. At Barrhill, the engines had to go through the goods shed to get the tail of the train clear. Sometimes a train had to be divided. On one occasion this was done at New Luce. Five coaches had to be put into the goods yard, so in obedience to grandmotherly old Board of Trade rules, the passengers in those coaches had to be taken out. The staff explained that it would only be for a short time, it was a fine day, so all hands got out on to the platform and sunned themselves. The 10.35am train drew past, the coaches were brought back from the yard, and then pandemonium, for no one could remember which compartment they had been in!

Yes, I felt very bitter about it. There were the other single-line, heavily-graded lines, the Highland, the Kyle of Lochalsh, the Oban, all well-equipped for passing-places, all with adequate motive power. Here we were, after 15 years of LMS administration, with no improvement on the Stranraer roads. Economy was now the grand, handy reply to any proposal for betterment. All those other lines had 4–6–0s. Stranraer could not turn them – a larger turntable could not be afforded. One Sunday in 1938 Kingmoor absentmindedly sent a Class 5X (Jubilee) 4–6–0 to Stranraer with an excursion for Larne. Stranraer had to turn out a pair of men to work it to Girvan for turning.

The annoying thing was that by then plenty of 4–6–0s were available. The first appeared on G&SW territory on through expresses about September 1933. These were what we called the Baby Scots, later the Patriot class. Kingmoor men used to bring them up, and they were grand engines. I always thought that they were the fastest 4–6–0s the LMS ever had. I always remember one day in 1943 when I was on the 5.30pm ex-St Enoch over the Barrhead road. We had a Baby Scot, No 5535, and a passed fireman driving who I do not think had been on one of the class before. Just as we went through Kilmaurs I recorded 80mph, or within a fraction of it, the highest I ever timed there. The young chap then braked, quite correctly, and ran the whole train, engine and eight coaches, through Kilmarnock No 1 home signal, standing red. The point was that he braked for what he took to be the usual 70mph, whereas it was 80mph, and that made all the difference. Some of the Kingmoor men were deceived also, and were found to be doing something like 80mph round the curves by Enterkinfoot, whereupon the engineer looked up his book and clapped a 55mph restriction on those curves which, in my experience, has been kept pretty rigidly since.

Then came what we called the Class 5Xs (I cannot even yet get used to the term 'Jubilee', and the Patriots were also in the same power class). I saw them quite early in their career, for I was on holiday at Crawford in August 1934 when those built by the North British Locomotive Co were coming up past in pairs, each pair hauled by a Caley 0–6–0. They went past to England and we saw them no more, but from my reading I gathered that they were giving quite a lot of bother. They began to work up the main line in 1935, and from their enginemen I heard of their shortcomings and was rather shocked. In the old days there had been classes which fell down largely from the imperfect knowledge of the time but now, with all the answers known, and a designer from Swindon, I just could not understand it. A Newton Heath fireman, leaving Glasgow Central with the 4.30pm, told me to watch the exhaust as they pulled out. Sure enough, in the centre of the column of white steam was the thin black column of water, like the lead in a pencil. Strangely, I never heard any particular reference to bad steaming with the class, but water – they were wading in it!

This was very disappointing, when the Baby Scots had been so good. Still, I heard that various experiments were being made to improve matters – domed boilers, bigger superheaters, removal of the jumper blastpipe. It was March of 1936 before any came to reside in our district. Nos 5575/6 came then to Corkerhill, and one Saturday when he was on the 1.16pm to Ayr I besought Bob Brown to open the smokebox door till I could count the superheater elements and check on the blastpipe. We got the door open to discover, of course, that our view was completely blocked by a wall of baffle plates! It was as big a surprise to the enginemen as it was to me.

Nos 5575/6 were definitely at Corkerhill, but Nos 5643–6 appeared frequently. I think that they were then at Kingmoor, but with those cyclic workings we began to pay less and less attention to code-plates on smokebox doors.

We soon learned that the stationing of Nos 5575/6 at Corkerhill was not a benevolent gesture towards the G&SW section. They were there to work a turn over the Caley. This was the 11.05pm from Glasgow Central to Liverpool and Manchester, and its working was given to Corkerhill top link. With one of those engines, or a substitute, they worked the 6.20pm to Ayr, came back to Glasgow with the 8.34pm, then ran the 11.05pm to Carlisle and booked-off. They returned next day, for a period, on the 3.13am, at another on the 4.20pm. The 11.05pm could be a heavy train. One night in summer Charlie Seivewright had No 5576 and 452 tons out of Central, without assistance. He was allowed 20 minutes to Motherwell and 28 minutes thence to Carstairs, at which place he was 5 minutes down, not bad work.

Sam Mitchell was on the 11.05pm one night. Jock Carnegie was firing and they had a Baby Scot. They got to Carstairs and found two firebars down and a lot of the fire in the ashpan. So they raked the fire out of the pan as they sat at the platform, while my friend Willie Robertson, then assistant inspector at Carstairs, tore his hair and lamented about his sleepers. 'Confound your sleepers,' says Mitchell (or words to that effect), 'we've got to get at the bars.' They managed to prop up the bars, took two big lumps off the tender and pushed them in as supports, then they got

Above: LMS Jubilee 4-6-0 No 5646 *Napier* at Corkerhill shed.
W. Potter

Below: Pinmore tunnel south end.
H. D. Bowtell

PINMORE TUNNEL
LENGTH 543 YARDS

Above: LMS 2P 4-4-0 No 644, then stationed at Hurlford, on a train to Ardrossan passing Perceton Junction.
F. R. Hebron

Below: LMS 2P 4-4-0 No 647 at Dalmellington, 1932.
D. L. Smith

away up the dark, stormy valley. Carnegie had never been over the road before. He wanted to keep a thick fire lest it burn down and set the supporting lumps alight, so he was forking in coal as hard as he could, but he got a bit tired and called out to Mitchell 'Are we anywhere near the summit yet?' 'Summit hell,' answered Mitchell, 'we're twelve mile down the far side!'

Christmas night of 1936 was a red-letter one for me. The Corkerhill top link had the 5.10pm, with 4–6–0s, and this was my first opportunity to time them. Sam Mitchell was on, with Tammy Borland firing and they had a Baby Scot No 5549, nominally of Polmadie. The load was a moderate 259 tons. As usual, the crew knew nothing of the engine's condition, save that one of the elements was blowing. The start was very ordinary, for we went slow road to Arkleston and had a bad permanent way slack at King Street, so by Beith we were $4\frac{1}{4}$ minutes down. Then the fun started. From a normal 66mph at Glengarnock, speed rose to 73mph at Dalry Junction, 77mph at Kilwinning, 79mph through Bogside, and just touched 80mph before Irvine – my one and only 80mph recording on a Glasgow–Ayr run! And now, when a compound would have been dropping into the lower 60s, this engine kept flying on, 77mph at Heatherhouse, 76mph at Barassie, 75mph at Troon Goods, 76mph at Prestwick and we took the curve from Falkland round through Newton station at 72mph! For all that, we did not quite manage it, arriving 35 seconds late.

A week later, on New Year's night, I tried again. Charlie Seivewright was driving this time, with No 5575, Ernie McCrindle firing, and a load of 289 tons. 'Very sore on water,' Charlie reported, 'she's throwing a lot out.' Our start out the Joint Line was not impressive. I could not see if the engine was throwing water, but she was certainly throwing *fire*. Steam seemed to be plentiful; No 5575 blew off several times. Charlie told me he was working in 15 per cent with full open regulator. We were a minute down at Beith, but then came an unfortunate signal check to 35mph at Swinlees. We recovered to 74mph by Irvine, but a heavy side wind and rain caught us and there were no records broken thereafter. We scrambled in five seconds early, which was certainly very accurate work.

The next great thought on the part of those who planned the cyclic workings was to give the 11.05pm Central–Carlisle to *Ayr* men! They had to run the 8.34pm to Glasgow, then the 11.05pm, book-off at Carlisle and return next day. Somewhere on the circuit they picked up a class 5X for the 11.05pm. It was a daft-like working, for the Ayr men's jobs had no link-up with those of the Caley main line. It was like giving Aberdeen men a job to Fort William. All six men had to start and learn the road, and learn it in the dark. I remember meeting Jimmy Cairns in Carlisle, worried and depressed by this heavy task thrust upon them. Of course the irrepressible Anthony Ross learned it in about two trips. He was on the 11.05pm one wild stormy night, and that night he had only a compound. As he flogged up towards the Summit he became aware of something black appearing and disappearing ahead of him. A boiler-band had slacked back and one of the cleading-sheets was flapping like a bat's wing! 'Gosh,' I said, 'where did you stop?' 'What would I stop for?' replied old Tony, 'It wasn't doin' me ony herm.' He was a hard case. This crazy working lasted for about six weeks, then the job went back to Corkerhill.

Ayr shed was in a spot of bother just then. The 7.46am to Glasgow had become a very important train, well filled by commuters who had to get to their business around 9.00am. The schedule, 41.4 miles in 64 minutes with six stops, was not just break-neck, but Ayr compounds could not time it, and Moguls did not seem to manage any better. I heard that increased power was to be provided for this train, and waited in pleased anticipation of a Class 5X or a Baby Scot. On 18 January 1937 there arrived at Ayr for the 7.46am Caledonian class 60 4–6–0 No 14641! I am not exaggerating when I say that of all classes of engine employed on main line express work at that time, none had a poorer reputation than the Caley 60s. My own runs behind them had been dull in the extreme. I knew an LMS official (ex-Caley) who commuted by the 7.46am, and in conversation ventured to hint that the authorities might have done something better for that train. He was shocked. 'Oh, but these are *grand* engines!' he protested. It is proof of my disinterest that I have no record whatever of No 14641's performance on this train. It did not remain at Ayr very long.

Talking of Ayr compounds reminds me of my old friend Johnnie McClymont who for quite a long time drove No 1181, and tended her with the greatest care. Johnnie was in at St Enoch one day when they came to him in desperation to see if he would pilot the up Thames–Clyde as far as Kilmarnock. 'Weel,' old Johnnie says, 'I hinna been ower the road since I was a fireman, but I daresay it's no' much altered.' So he backed on to a Baby Scot and a big English driver comes forward swinging the cloth. 'Now driver,' he says, 'this is a hard job. You've got to *run* on this job.' 'Aye, aye,' replies old Johnnie, 'on ye go. I'll be there afore ye.'

At the end of March 1939 there came momentous news – official sanction for a 60ft turntable for Stranraer; 4–6–0s to work to Stranraer over both routes . . . I sometimes wonder if the LMS got a government ultimatum. Certainly without that 60ft table I do not see how the terrific wartime traffic at Stranraer could ever have been handled.

7

The Second World War

And now, having neglected the Stranraer routes for 16 years, the LMS authorities could not wait. As early as 23 March 1939 they had staged a test load with a Class 5 4–6–0, on the 8.49am ex-Glasgow and the 4.20pm ex-Stranraer carrying a 260-ton load south of Girvan. No 5454 was the engine – I expect that they had to separate engine and tender at Stranraer to get them turned. I heard that the trial was very successful, especially when, with the load increased to 295 tons, they raced up from Girvan to Maybole in 15 minutes, the boiler being nearly emptied in the process. There was no prospect of the 60ft turntable being ready before late summer, so they laid longer rails, projecting at each end, on the existing 50ft turntable. This allowed them to turn a Class 5 4–6–0, but there could not have been much margin, and a Class 5X was out meantime. The Class 5s began to work from Glasgow to Stranraer on 16 April 1939.

We had not seen much of those Class 5 4–6–0s on the Ayr lines. They worked in on the Perth goods, and that was about all. The official term was 4–6–0 5P5F, which was rather a mouthful. I saw that enthusiasts in England were calling them 'Black Fives'. 'Black' was not much of a distinction among Scottish engines, whether by paint or dirt or both.

They sent us five of the class for the new working: Nos 5178, 5179, 5319, 5357 and 5467. They were a bright bunch. No 5467 was reported to be 'not so bad'; the rest were knocking, more or less violently, in the left-hand trailing axlebox. No 5179 did one trip and had to go to the shops; No 5178 was laid aside for works. No 5357 was so atrocious that both Sam Mitchell and Jimmy McCreadie refused to take it out. No 5319 was put onto a

94

'Hellifield job' which Corkerhill had at that time; No 5467 was purloined by Kingmoor. However, the workshops gave them a lick and a promise, the stragglers were rounded-up, and the enginemen learned to live with the knock. Girvan men got the 5.10pm that summer, and they used to come in standing on the tender footplate to ease their legs.

The test run with the class 5 on 23 March had a rather amusing sequel. There was still at Northern Division headquarters a hard core of ex-Caley men. They appeared to feel slighted at this new 4–6–0 class being preferred for the Stranraer road over their incomparable 60 class 4–6–0s, so on 26 April another test was carried out with the same 8.49am and 4.20pm, engine No 14633 of Polmadie, with Stranraer and Ayr men. I was promised a log of this test, but never got it. Maybe it was just as well.

One evening in mid-May I was returning from Stranraer on the 7.13pm with No 5319 and the usual three coaches. At New Luce I was bidden to the footplate and given the driver's seat, but not for long. At every revolution of the wheels there came a violent kick in the pants! I rose rather hurriedly – I had never felt anything like it. I was assured that this was 'a *good* one. You should try such-and-such a one.' With three coaches one could play about a bit. We tried that engine all sorts of ways – full open, big valve, just open, small valve, 30 per cent, 20 per cent – but we just could not cut out that knock. It was a strange engine. With only three on, one would have thought that full open and 25 per cent would have been ample even for the steep climb at 1 in 57 to the Swan's Neck. We just managed 11 minutes to Glenwhilly with nothing to spare. From Pinwherry up the 1 in 65/7 to Pinmore we tried her in 30 per cent and the small valve a little way open. It flew up, almost too hard for the curves. From Girvan with six coaches it went up Killochan on 30 per cent and small valve well open, cut back to 25 per cent at the top, and it tore up to Maybole in 16½ from Girvan faster than I had come *down* sometimes.

As a great favour, we were allowed to keep the 'test' Caley, and No 14633 went into the circuit with the Fives. There were some pithy comments. Mulholland on Caley 60s was worth hearing.

Then one night I went up to see the 8.05pm ex-Glasgow and in with No 14633 came Sam Mitchell. I approached gingerly, awaiting a torrent of vituperation surpassing all others. 'Do you know,' said Mitchell, 'this engine has some *speed* in her. She's a devil to go!'

What was one to make of that? A fortnight later I went to Glasgow on the 1.52pm ex-Ayr, No 14633 with Billy Sloan ('The Herd') of Girvan, and 319 tons. Willie Dummigan was firing. We got away rapidly, through Troon Goods in 8 minutes 48 seconds, and were doing 66mph at Gailes (most exceptional) when came signals. To cut it short, we did the 33.7 miles to Paisley in a net time of 34¾ minutes (36 booked). It was a splendid piece of work, far better than I had been used to with the compounds. Certainly the old Herd was a hard hitter, but I was well forward in the train and did not hear much of the exhaust. To compare, Sam McKnight of Girvan was on this train with No 5467 and 349 tons. He told me that he had her in 30 per cent with full open regulator, and he took 37 minutes net to Paisley. Speed hung at 58mph for a long way, and touched 61mph as a maximum. Sam's brother Sandy had No 5319 and 323 tons, Ned McWhirter firing. Speeds were certainly higher than with No 5467, but net time to Paisley was not under 36 minutes.

This was all very perplexing. I studied No 14633 for some time. There were various opinions. Then one Sunday evening she was on the 8.05pm with 'Sprig' – James Thomson of Stranraer. He came tearing in from Glasgow with only six coaches and ran two past the platform in desperation to get to the water column, the tender tank being dry. The 60s had a tender capacity of 4,200 gallons. A good compound or Mogul could do Glasgow–Girvan on 1,500 gallons. There was something not too good about them. After about three weeks of the Stranraer turns No 14633 was in a state of filth that beggared description. If the injector went off you could not get it back on until she stopped. Jimmy McGee had No 14633 on the 8.05pm one night. Half the brick arch was down and tubes were blowing. He stopped at Johnstone and exchanged No 14633 for another 60, No 14646 off a goods train. It did quite well, McGee reported, but was very sore on water. The crew which took No 14633 light to Corkerhill had to stop at Hawkhead to get the boiler filled!

Yes, it *was* very puzzling. I began to wonder if the Caley men had been working the 60s the wrong way. Caley runs had shown no evidence of any capacity for speed, yet here were our G&SW men, when the engines were in reasonable order, getting good work out of them. By 1939, Corkerhill and Ayr men were becoming quite accustomed to Caleys, mainly 4–4–0s. They had even got used to that super-Caley atrocity, the steam reverser. You lifted the latch on the big hand lever, then stooped down behind it to apply the steam, whereupon the lever came back and hit you on the side of the head. Goods drivers and firemen had learned to accept those crazy footplate arrangements where the driver stood on the right-hand side working the regulator and steam brake, while the fireman on the left side worked the reverser. They *had* to accept them, for there were now no G&SW engines left! Certainly a few Drummond 2–6–0s lingered about Corkerhill, but down the Ayr road the fine products of Manson and Smellie seemed now as remote as Stephenson's *Rocket*.

It was a strange, uneasy summer, that of 1939, with the threat of war hanging over us. It seemed to affect everything. The Irish traffic via Stranraer, my particular interest, had somehow lost its spring. This may have been due to the fact that having now got more adequate power for the Stranraer road, the LMS began cutting loads. At the period of the Glasgow Fair in mid-July, certainly, a type of passenger regulation was in force. Trains were limited to, say, 10 or 11 coaches, and passengers directed to certain trains. There was now adequate seating accommodation, but more trains and more stock were required, and some of the stock was rather awful. In particular, there were many coaches without corridors or lavatory facilities, a very undesirable feature on a journey of maybe $3\frac{1}{2}$ hours, for stops at Ayr and Girvan were often brief, station toilets were quite inadequate, and at Ayr were reached by traversing a ticket barrier and walking some distance beyond.

So here I was, in the summer to which I had looked forward, with 4–6–0s on the Stranraer road at last – and I could not have cared less. Ten-coach trains and pilots, pilots, pilots; there was little interest in it all. I gave up my annual pilgrimage to Stranraer on Glasgow Fair Saturday evening. Not that the Fives were very prominent. Here is a list of up trains observed at Ayr on Fair Friday, 14 July 1939:

	Locomotive	Coaches	Pilot from Ayr
9.00am to Stranraer	5179	12	4182
Relief to 10.35am	914	10	4258
Relief to 10.35am	1080	9	4259
10.35am to Stranraer Hbr.	1179	9	—
Relief to 3.50pm	617/915	9	—
Relief to 3.50pm	1130	9	—
Relief to Girvan	4323	7	—
3.50pm to Stranraer Harbour	2834	11	2807
Relief to Girvan	2908	8	—
8.05pm to Stranraer Harbour	5357	12	4258

I had managed a short holiday to the Lake District, and returned on Sunday 9 July, changing at Carlisle to the 10.30am ex-St Pancras. Our steed for the G&SW section was to be that enigmatic engine No 5467, in charge of two young enthusiasts from Corkerhill, who promised me a run of surpassing brilliance. They had every inducement, for the 10.30am came in 28 minutes late, with No 1006 and a badly-burned smokebox door. The load was 294 tons from Carlisle. We set off, and I could only describe the journey to Dumfries as poor in the extreme. There was not a sparkle anywhere. It was the same going up the Nith valley: 45mph minimum on the 1 in 150 to the tunnel and 42 minutes 40 seconds to pass New Cumnock were very ordinary figures. But then things started. We came round Cumnock curve at $77\frac{1}{2}$mph, and 74mph on the level to Auchinleck, 77½mph at the Barony, 80mph Brackenhill, 82mph over Ballochmyle, 83½mph before Mauchline, 72mph at the tunnel, 75mph Garrochburn, 84mph and then brakes for an adverse distant signal at Hurlford! 21.2 miles New Cumnock to Kilmarnock, in 17¾ minutes net — it was my record for the course until I timed the headlong descent of a Sulzer in the early days of diesels.

Then quite suddenly war was upon us. On 1 September the Evacuation specials began, but of those I saw very little. It was a great fiasco in our district. Hardly one-quarter of the expected numbers turned up; some trains were cancelled, but the majority were run as scheduled, to result in a congestion down Stranraer way never seen before. Of those happenings I can give few details; I was careful and troubled about many other things. It was not until months after that I heard some of the grisly tales, of trains or light engines held up on crossing loops, sometimes for hours, of crews running out of food — one crew ate turnips out of an adjacent field — of cases of overtime never seen since the days of the Other War.

I did not go much to Ayr station those nights — blacked-out, one or two dim blue lights, sandbags, and over the footplates of my friends' engines that smothering anti-glare sheet. It was a daunting place of an evening, with little groups of young soldiers leaving — strained, frightened faces, and women, quietly weeping in dark corners. To me, who could remember the departures of the first world war, the cheering, the confident boasting, the flag-waving, it was really frightening. We knew about war now, perhaps not a bad thing, but it did not make easy the departure of those who had to go and fight it.

So for a time my notes of railway happenings are rather scanty. Only gradually did I learn of the sweeping changes in engine locations. Ayr lost its compounds, its moguls, its Class 4Fs. In their place we got a steady influx of Class 2P 4—4—0s, until there were 17 at Ayr; for goods work, of course, Caley 18in and 18½in 0—6—0s. It was about October that the new 60ft turntable was ready at Stranraer, and at once all our Fives were swept away. I next saw No 5319 at *Elgin* in 1945, with a Forres driver in charge.

As replacements came Class 5Xs, and those were to be the mainstay of the Stranraer road throughout the war. I cannot give a tidy list of those which came, but Nos 5643–6 appeared frequently, and so did Nos 5713–6. Great variety arose from the down Paddy from Carlisle being worked by a Crewe North engine. This, during its 14 hours at Stranraer, worked the 11.41am to Glasgow and the 5.10pm back. I do not propose to quote any names for the class 5Xs; I found that the enginemen paid little or no attention to the names. The only exception that I remember was a Stranraer man who referred to No 5732 *Sanspareil* as 'Aul' Sarsaparilla'.

Corkerhill had been losing its compounds, Moguls, and Class 5s, and in their place came the Caley 60s! Corkerhill had eventually 10, and they were distinctly 'not amused'. As I have indicated, the 60s, with careful attention, under 'G&SW management' so to speak, had been showing some very encouraging results, but it was wartime now. There was no time for careful treatment by top-link men. They were pitched about from hand to hand, thrown onto the Stranraer jobs with maybe a passed fireman and a cleaner. There developed a hatred of the breed and the forging of that infamous nickname 'The Greybacks'. The name may have arisen from the normal appearance in wartime: the long boiler-top, unbroken by a Belpaire firebox, filthy black and powdered by the white ash of a few fire-cleanings. Of course, the term was also applied to a louse, which most Corkerhill men would have thought very appropriate.

By 1938 the economy drive on the LMS was going very strongly, and those responsible were determined that neither wars nor rumours of wars would stay their progress. In January 1939, with war clouds very dark on the horizon, they succeeded in wiping out the key signal-box of Challoch Junction. It was replaced by a very novel and complicated electrical system worked from Dunragit, a system quite liable to complete failure at a critical time. A useful little crossing-loop was also abolished. Then for a long time Economy had had its eye on Girvan, and with all this wartime traffic ahead, they struck on 4 February

1940. This happy little shed, which had done such yeoman service on the heavy road to the south, was suddenly reduced to a subshed of Ayr, in nominal charge of a foreman fitter. Three engines stayed there overnight, but they were only birds of passage. Seven pairs of enginemen were left, but there was terrible upheaval. Two express drivers, men of near 60 years of age, were back to firing. Ten younger men were moved to other depots, but some left railway service in disgust — good men whose experience would have been of great value in the dark days ahead. Tammy McCrindle joined his family in the fishing trade. We might have known that this was only the beginning of the end for Girvan. On 1 March 1941 the shed was finally closed. All had to go then. The older men were uprooted also. Most went to Ayr, but Sandy McKnight alone went to Stranraer. It was not easy, for he landed in the top link, and had to learn the 100 miles from Challoch Junction to Carlisle, and learn it in the dark and the blackout. He did splendid work, but it was a big strain, and when a vacancy arose towards the end of the war he was not averse to going on an easier pilot job.

All this time we in south-west Scotland had suffered no trouble through enemy action, but on Sunday 28 January 1940 disruption struck, but not from enemy action, just the forces of nature — a snowfall such as had not been seen for a century! It was snowing gently on the Saturday night, with a little lying underfoot, but on Sunday we woke to a white world. In the afternoon came a furious blizzard and by dark we were drifted-up.

Ayr shed got snow ploughs ready, engine No 17271 with the big plough and No 17364 with the small one, the engines coupled tender-to-tender. Drivers were Davie Cuthbert and Willie Wilson respectively. They got away for the south about noon. With some heavy ploughing they won through to New Luce about 4.00pm. There they learned that the fancy electrical set-up at Challoch Junction was out for the count and they could get no further. By this time the line behind them was drifted-up solid, so there they were, marooned in New Luce — four enginemen, a ganger, two fitters and two inspectors. They kept steam in the engines until

9.00am on the Monday and had then to draw the fires. All put up at the little hotel in the village and were there till the following Wednesday, when Stranraer ploughs got through to them. They could not go north, so went to Stranraer where they lodged in the 'Buck's Head' and worked from Stranraer, mainly working on the Girvan line, until Monday 5 February, when snow ploughs from the north at last got through. A 15ft drift at the Swan's Neck took a bit of shifting.

Meanwhile, work had been going on to the north. When the storm started on the Sunday, Girvan got its snow plough out with two engines on it. They managed to burst through the big cut before Killochan, but could get no further, and as they were blocked behind, they put the engines into Killochan yard, dumped the fires and walked home.

Later on the Sunday, Ayr got out another snow plough, with two engines tail-to-tail. They left some time in the afternoon, got through to Kilkerran, but Ben's Cut was full by this time; they drove into it up to the neck and stuck fast. They managed to keep steam in one engine and Eddie Barlow stood by all night. Dougie Gibson, Kilkerran stationmaster, carried up dry boots and socks for him. The Gibsons had two stranded passengers as lodgers that night; one was the daughter of a lighthouse-keeper, on her way to Ailsa Craig!

On the Monday they got a work train down to Kilkerran. They tried to pull the embedded engine and snow plough out with a tail rope, but the rope broke and they had to send to Ayr for chains. They worked till midnight and eventually cleared Ben's Cut, but the big cut south of Killochan was a worse job. They tackled that on the Tuesday, working until dusk and then returning to Irvine. No 14445 was tender-first and Jock Livingston was so cold that he left the train on the main line at Ayr No 2 signalbox, and went inside to turn the locomotive, with the Maybole–Glasgow passenger train sitting 20 minutes at Belmont behind him. They got through to Girvan on Wednesday, 31 January.

All this time everything out of Ayr was blocked except Maybole, Glasgow and Kilmarnock. By Monday evening, however, snow blown off the fields had filled the rock cut at Drybridge; the 6.43pm from Kilmarnock ran into it and was stuck for two hours. Kilmarnock–Dumfries had been hopeless from the start; there were stories of four engines up to the chimney-top in a cut near Cumnock. Dalmellington and Rankinston were both blocked, and of course Ayr–Muirkirk. We heard that no wheel had turned on the Dumfries–Stranraer line.

It must have been a tremendous task, but they were getting through. They ploughed to Waterside on the Tuesday and so got the coal traffic moving. On the Friday, 2 February, the first train got through to Dumfries and Carlisle. Next day they got the Port Road opened. So it went on but it was Thursday 8 February before Ayr–Muirkirk was cut through, and even then only single-line between Muirkirk and Cronberry.

Inspector McCaig of Ayr told me of some adventures of the Ayr snow ploughs. He was out with a two-engine outfit on the Dalmellington line. They were much hampered by the driver of the leading engine. He was apparently nervous, and would shut off as they approached each drift. Next they went on the Turnberry road. The leading driver must have got a tonic, for they went out through Dunure station thunder-and-turf, banged into a big drift in the narrow cut to the south, and sent up a perfect torrent of snow. Unfortunately a citizen of Dunure had his greenhouse on the rim of the cut and the snow, descending, broke seven panes of glass. They tore on and into the bigger rock cut below Dunure Mains, but this was too much. They stuck dead and were not hauled out for 36 hours.

A most extraordinary feature of this Big Snow was the blocking of the Ardrossan–Largs line. As far as I am aware, this had never happened before. There was no rail or road communication with that area for about ten days. Commuters to Glasgow went by steamer from Largs to Gourock, whence the Caley line to Glasgow was open. The Storm Demon seemed to have vented his especial rage upon Fairlie tunnel. The southern portal was completely blocked. Ardrossan would not be first priority for a snow plough, but on 3 February they got one. They put three engines on to it, Nos 17348, 4251 and 17300 and went off on a wild charge. They got into the tunnel and raced on, only to crash into a hard pillar of snow which had gathered under a ventilation shaft. All three engines were derailed; in the smoke and steam and darkness Alf Burdon, driver of the leading engine, got down from the footplate, tripped and fell heavily, sustaining fatal injuries. It was Wednesday, 7 February before they got the first passenger train through to Largs, full service being resumed two days later.

So we struggled clear of the snow, rather thankful that the enemy had not chosen that moment to attack us, for roads were blocked even worse than railways. I got down to Stranraer on Saturday, 10 February, and found it like a city after a siege. They had even been bringing yeast by air from Belfast to make bread!

The Big Snow over, entries in my notebook become rather scanty again. I record that on 6 April 1940 the 9.55pm Paddy out of Stranraer Harbour for London was loaded to six first-class sleepers and eleven corridor coaches, 547 tons tare. Sam Balfour of Stranraer had a Class 5X, with a Class 2P 4—4—0 piloting; they must have had a heavy pull to get over Gatehouse with that load.

The Port Road was soon doing a prodigious job. I know now of the 36 troop trains that traversed it in that same month of April as our forces were built up in Northern Ireland against the possibility of the Germans invading Eire. Only vague rumours of such happenings reached my ears, nothing to record in a notebook, and then by May 1940 our whole world was toppling about our ears. It was a grim time, and I am not a very heroic person, but never shall I forget that wonderful speech of Churchill in the House of Commons on 18 June. From my mood of numb despair I was raised to a new hope and confidence. By July I was taking an interest in railway matters once more, just in time to take notes of the accident on the Stranraer road which happened in the very early morning of 12 July 1940.

The train concerned was once more the 6.35pm, Stranraer to Glasgow goods, but an account of its make-up and dispatch will give some idea of the press of wartime traffic at Stranraer. The time of departure was still nominally 6.35pm, but by the departure time of the Glasgow Paddy, 9.35pm, the goods had not got away, so they kept it to follow the Paddy, which left about 10.50pm. What should have hauled the goods I know not, but all they could get was a Class 2P 4–4–0 No 642 belonging to Dumfries. The Corkerhill man was a passed fireman, Bob Kerr. He had come recently to Corkerhill from Hurlford and did not know the Stranraer route, so he had as conductor a passed fireman from Ayr, Andy ('Spark') McMurtrie. Then Davie Stevenson of Corkerhill had been to Stranraer with a troop train and was working home, so he piloted the goods with Class 4F 0–6–0 No 4316, which I think was at that time a Perth engine. They had a train of 30 wagons and got other seven at Dunragit.

They stopped at Barrhill and both engines took water, then they went on and about 12.45am were descending through the rock cutting at the Bents farm when there was an almighty crash in the rear. They pulled up and went back to investigate, to be met at the mouth of the cut by a rush of terrified swine from their smashed cattle wagons. The cut was almost full of the debris of their train and on top of all the wreckage of the wooden footbridge which here spanned the cut.

Davie Stevenson cut loose and took his engine to Pinwherry with the tablet. The outside world was informed. The Girvan tool van came up, and in the fulness of time the cranes, the Motherwell one from the north, and the Kingmoor one from the south. Actually, Kingmoor had to do the lion's share, for the Motherwell crane was hampered badly by an overhead pipeline which spanned the cut. They did very well, for the line was clear for the 8.05pm from St Enoch and the Paddy that same night, though the 8.05pm had to be held 65 minutes at Pinwherry for the Motherwell crane working.

Of course it had to be the morning of Glasgow Fair Saturday. Three single-deck buses were procured from Scottish Motor Traction, also Gibbie Templeton's bus from Ballantrae and two lorries for luggage. Those ferried passengers and belongings between Pinwherry and Barrhill stations. Class 5X No 5636 worked the 8.45am ex-St Enoch, with Harry Barr of Corkerhill. Sanny Taylor of Ayr relieved him and ran to Pinwherry and back to Girvan. There he turned and ran to Glasgow, returning on the 5.10pm. Joe Glendinning relieved him at Ayr and ran to Pinwherry, and back tender-first with the empty coaches. That night it was discovered that no one had oiled No 5636 all day!

By chance I was on Ayr platform when the train crew of the wrecked 6.35pm arrived for the official inquiry. I was surrounded by half-a-dozen men all trying to tell their stories at once. 'The brig cam' doon on the tap o' us!' was the burden of their lay. I commiserated with them and wished them well at the inquiry. This I gathered later, went well, with no blame to anyone.

In sorting out the wreckage, a broken axle was found on one of the wagons. The authorities had been a little puzzled about a collapsing bridge causing such an accident. Why should it collapse? Here was probably a more likely cause.

On the following Monday morning, Andy Bowman of Girvan piloted the 9.00am goods to New Luce. He was coming back light when just north of the Chirmorie houses some surfacemen stopped him and asked if he would take down to Girvan something that they had found on the line – a wagon drawbar. Evidently the 6.35pm had broken away about milepost 15¼. With the guard holding tight in the rear, the two portions either stopped separately in Barrhill station or came together so gently that no one noticed. When he heard the engines restart, the guard released his brake and his portion followed by gravity. Goods men usually started to brake about the Bents. If they slowed up the first portion the second would overtake. It was quite a study in cause and effect. The crew told me that they shut off as they came over the Chirmorie. That, I used to be told, was wrong. There was a little bit of level at the Chirmorie houses. If you were running without steam, the wagons would pile up on the engines on that level, then as the engines tipped over the edge of the 1 in 80, bang would go the couplings.

This was the only serious accident on the Girvan–Stranraer section during the war, a very creditable record for all concerned.

Above: LMS 2P 4-4-0 No 667 (Ardrossan shed) at Paisley (Gilmour Street) with a train to Glasgow.
L. Hanson

Below: LMS No 14161, Manson 8 class 4-4-0 ex G&SW 73/414.
J. B. Aird

Above: Glasgow–Girvan train at Newton-on-Ayr. LMS 4-4-0 No 14333, ex Caledonian No 777.
D. L. Smith collection

Below: Southbound train rounding lower curve of Swan's Neck.
E. M. Patterson

8

Total War

One of the primary duties of a railway in wartime is to move troops, and the LMS in south-west Scotland got its full share of this task. Unfortunately those interesting happenings were hush-hush; they often took place when I was either working or sleeping, so my records are scanty. As early as 1 December 1939, I noted that Ernie McCrindle stuck on the Swan's Neck with a train of troops from Ireland, 4.40am, from Stranraer Harbour with engine No 1080 and 182 tons. He had to divide the train, and was two hours late by Ayr. There was nothing very new in this; it had been done before, in both wars.

On 11 October 1940, about 8.30pm, a troop train en route to Stranraer stopped for water at Girvan. The troops had left Kyle of Lochalsh at 4.30am, and would be pretty tired by the time they reached destination, probably somewhere in Northern Ireland. They had a Class 5X and nine coaches on. Sam McKnight banked them to Milepost $3\frac{3}{4}$.

One day in that same October Willie Cranston of Ayr was given Class 5X No 5582 and a train of eight corridors and sent to Happendon, between Muirkirk and Lanark. 9,000 Polish troops were being moved from camps in Douglasdale to stations on or near the East coast. There were 14 troop trains, and Willie's was the second to last, with Forfar as its destination. Willie knew the road to Carstairs, but he was given a conductor at Lanark Racecourse, then it was non-stop to Stirling, where they arrived 15 minutes early at 2.00am. There the Ayr men and their engine were relieved, to take their statutory rest, but with a wet, cold night and no provision for their shelter, they were glad to see the last of Stirling about noon and to take No 5582 back to Ayr.

Apparently they were an engine short for this move, for the last troop train was made up to 16 corridors, and its engine was compound No 1126! Control found a man at Douglas West who piloted them to Cleghorn, after which the compound went off to Stirling alone with its train. They would do it all right – compounds were astonishing engines.

We were still getting compounds on the Stranraer line, but the main force was composed of Class 5Xs. An occasional Baby Scot showed up again; the first that I saw was No 5523 on 5 October 1940. Crewe North began to slip an occasional Royal Scot into Stranraer with the Carlisle Paddy. On 7 December 1940 I noted that George Hannay of Stranraer had three Royal Scots on the Paddy that week, Nos 6108, 6115 and 6124. The Stranraer men got on all right with the Royal Scots, but thought them heavy on coal. For some reason they were not permitted on the Stranraer–Girvan route.

On 6 December 1940 there blew a terrible gale. The 1.00am goods had a Greyback piloted by a Caley 0–6–0, and took 70 minutes for the $8\frac{1}{2}$ miles from Barrhill to Glenwhilly. The 7.05am passenger from Stranraer, with a Class 5X and five coaches, took 65 minutes from Girvan to Ayr (schedule 37), slipping all the way. The 2.45pm Ayr to Stranraer goods stuck on Glendoune despite having a Class 5X piloted by a class 2P. Sandy McKnight, into Ayr with No 598, was dispatched to Glasgow as the 9.00am. He had to come almost to a stop at Barassie, unable to see signals owing to hail and spindrift. He lost only three minutes to Glasgow, however.

Large numbers of troops were now stationed in Northern Ireland, and the ordinary passenger service proved quite inadequate for men going on leave to England and Wales. A special sailing had to be provided, with two large trains in connection. A train from London and one from Cardiff worked into Stranraer in the early morning, returning in the evening about 6.30pm. These were made up eventually to 16 coaches, each with a buffet car. Siding accommodation at Stranraer was terribly inadequate. They could service only one of those huge trains, so the Cardiff train had to be hauled to Ayr and back each day for servicing. Two Caley Class 3F 0–6–0s were put on this job, but even so they had to be banked up Glendoune by a Class 2F 0–6–0 from Girvan shed. On 1 March 1941 the wiseacres closed Girvan shed, and apparently nothing powerful enough could be found to eliminate banking. So two of the 'River' class 4–6–0s which F. G. Smith had built for the Highland Railway in 1915 were literally taken from the scrap-heap and sent to Ayr for this work.

Nos 14758 and 14760, that was the pair. No 14760 was trailing an eight-wheeled 'centipede' tender of Drummond design off a Highland 'Castle', which did not improve its beauty. Both locomotives were in a horrible state. I first saw them on 3 March 1941, with two Ayr men, Geordie Hewitson and Jock Jardine. Hewitson had no leathers in his steam reverser. Eventually both got Smith tenders, which looked a little neater. They were very high engines, and John McCormack put his head out to see if the anti-glare sheet had got entangled, whereupon his head hit a bridge near Castle Kennedy. The speed may be judged by the fact that he was off duty for a fortnight only. I took a note from several guards' journals; three hours was the fastest time I recorded for the 58½ miles Stranraer to Ayr.

By this time the country round Stranraer was becoming fairly populated by service establishments, but on 20 January 1941 there began the biggest of all the activities in that district. Plans had been prepared even before the war for the construction of two new ports in quiet districts of western Scotland, to be brought into use should either Liverpool or Glasgow suffer crippling bomb damage. Military Port No 1 was to be at Faslane, on Gareloch; Port No 2 was to be at Cairnryan, about 6½ miles north of Stranraer, on the east shore of Loch Ryan. Work began on the Cairnryan port on 20 January 1941. A siding from the main line was laid in one mile east of Stranraer Harbour Junction, and controlled by a ground frame. The first occupants of the siding were five dormitory coaches and a canteen van, for which train an ex-Highland 4–4–0 LMS No 14382 *Loch Moy* supplied steam heat, though minus its internal machinery. This siding expanded into a large yard of ten parallel roads, and from it the Cairnryan Military Railway, ultimately 6¼ miles long, curved round to the shore of the loch. There were some very extensive railway layouts on the course of the CMR, but of those I saw little or nothing during the period of their working. My visits to Stranraer were mostly somewhat brief and occupied in research into much more ancient activity.

I did however see certain of the line's working at the junction. A signalbox was erected there and opened on 11 October 1942. The first of the WD engines which I saw here was ex-Great Western Railway Dean Goods No 2470; later there came a great variety of engines – the J69s of the LNER were numerous, and I have a note of seven of the Dean Goods. All I got was a passing glance. I daresay that had I travelled by bus to Stranraer I could have seen a great deal, but there was plenty else to see by rail and I was content.

Traffic to this new port was very nearly the last straw for the two main lines approaching Stranraer. How the traffic had been handled up to that time I just do not know. Loops, some with a capacity of no more than an engine and eight coaches, and trains of two engines and sixteen – 'crossing' stations still prohibited from crossing two passenger trains – loops, some at the foot of steep gradients, with a speed restriction of 15mph for non-stopping trains. For Control, it must have been Frustration with a capital F. At last, something was done. All loops were lengthened to accord with the Glenwhilly arrangement of 1937. Capacity aimed at was, I understand, two engines and twelve coaches. But just when they might have done the job thoroughly they stuck, blinded by their old theory that a crossing point must have up and down roads, this at a time when single lines all over the world were laying out their crossing points with one road straight, for non-stopping trains in both directions, and the other road looped for stopping trains, splendidly carried out no further away than the NCC system, which itself was part of the LMS domain, in Northern Ireland. No, it had to be up and down roads, but to help matters, great and no doubt expensive long-bladed points were installed at each end, and speed limits raised to 50mph.

Maybe it was just as well, for the Bryson tablet exchange apparatus was now installed on the Port Road as well as the Girvan line. The tablet catchers on the locomotives were certainly massive things now, but the big hoops remained; they were heavy enough to look at, but I do not think they would have stood up to use at more than 50mph. It was sad to think of the excellent Manson catcher, given up by the Port Road after the first world war, a catcher which I have seen doing its exchanging at speeds up to 76mph.

The advantage claimed for the Bryson catcher was that it was portable; the big heavy head fitted into a socket on the side of the cab. Wartime working found it just too portable! If booked for a Stranraer job and there was no catcher on the engine, nor any in the store, it was a case of just stealing one off another engine. Regular crews took to locking-up their catchers in the toolbox. Quite often you had to go off without a catcher, in which case tablets were exchanged by hand. You held your arm level and parallel with the cab-side, the hoop dangling beneath your hand. The hook on the ground apparatus took the hoop out of your hand and your arm went straight on through the incoming hoop. It was a case of holding steady and hoping the driver would not go too hard, for the hoops were heavy. One night in the autumn of 1941, Will Irvine The Pumper was on the Paddy with a young lad firing. They had no catcher, and at Pinwherry the hook went up the boy's sleeve and walloped him out on to the platform. He was a bit shaken, but said he could go on. Sandy McKnight was going home for the weekend and he went on the footplate with them to Girvan. Another night John McGuire was on the milk empties to Stranraer. He had a catcher all right, and at Cairnryan Junction it not only caught the tablet but part of the ground equipment as well and pulled the whole apparatus out by the roots. Unfortunately the lady signalman was standing on the footboard of the apparatus so she must have got a bit of an upheaval.

Several of the Stranraer line signal boxes had lady 'signalmen' during the war. The girls did very well, but they were a little

113

annoying at times. When the passing loops were extended, the home signals were put further out, which meant that most of the distant signals also had to be put further out; some of them were nearly a mile from the signal box. That was a heavy pull; some of the girls decided it was *too* heavy so they just didn't pull-off the distants at all. This could cause slight delay to a non-stop passenger train, but to a non-fitted goods it was disastrous, creeping in for over a mile, holding hard in case it was not clear right through.

I think that the classic story of the signalwomen time is that which is related of Glenwhilly. The train was the 4.20pm from Stranraer, and just as it got dark it was running into the down platform at Glenwhilly. Usually the girl would be standing on the platform with the tablet, but that evening she was a bit late; as they ran in, she came down the stairs on to the up platform. To save her crossing over, the fireman threw his tablet to her, and she threw hers to him, but he missed his catch and it fell into the six-foot. As soon as they stopped he got down and went back to retrieve it. The hoop was retrieved at once, but alas the pouch had burst open and the tablet gone. The fireman went back for a lamp, and made a long search, but in vain. There was nothing for it but to inform Control. Control would arrange for Barrhill ($8\frac{1}{4}$ miles away) to provide a pilotman. They telephoned Barrhill. 'Pilotman!' cried the solitary porter. 'What d'you think I am? It's Saturday afternoon an' I'm here by masel'. I can dae nithing for ye.' Too bad, so they then called Pinwherry ($12\frac{1}{2}$ miles). I do not think the staff was any more numerous there, but the stationmaster (off duty) was in his house adjacent; he said that he would officiate and called up a taxi. It was going to be a long, cold wait, so the fireman went up into the signalbox, and the girl made him a cup of tea. Now the fireman was a voracious reader, and he found the signalbox a perfect treasure-house. Old McGibney had been a bit of a magpie – his cupboards were crammed with books and magazines and papers dating back to the erection of that box in 1907. The fireman read until his eyes were sore, then he had a stroll around. He lifted the lock of the tablet instrument and pulled out the slide – and there was the missing tablet. In her hurry the girl had grabbed the hoop and forgotten that she had never put the tablet in the pouch! I never heard the sequel to that one, and I had not the nerve to ask!

It was while they were lengthening the loops that Pinmore, of all places, had a nasty little smash. Pinmore had only a single platform, on the up line; the down line was a loop for goods trains only. Off the goods loop there was a small two-road yard. During the war, a goods train left Stranraer in the morning and worked to Girvan, returning from there at 1.00pm. That day Hughie Murray ('The Lintie') of Stranraer was on it, with Class 5X No 5731. They had only eleven wagons and van back from Girvan; they went racing up to the tunnel in 12 minutes and emerged from it at a much higher speed than usual. At Pinmore there was a train waiting at the platform, so they were signalled into the loop, but as they came round the curve, braking, but still going hard, the signalman had to think, and think quickly. They would go on to the loop all right, but they would not be able to stop before they got to its south end. There they would derail at the trap points, the big, heavy engine would probably slew round and hit the side of the standing train. It was a choice of evils, so the signalman turned the goods train into the yard. There they encountered two wagons and a dormitory coach for the men working at the loop. No 5731 demolished the lot – the coach fortunately unoccupied at the time – the Stranraer crew baled out and escaped injury. The breakdown train, comprising the steam crane from Hurlford, soon arrived. It was sitting on the goods loop with engine attached; the foreman wanted a shift 'Just a wee bit. Woa!' The coupling, unoiled and stiff, rose off the hook and away ran the crane, to derail at the trap points, slew round, and block both roads. The Motherwell crane had to come to rerail the Hurlford one!

The most congested part of the approaches to Stranraer was the 6.4 miles from Challoch Junction to Harbour Junction, which had to carry the traffic both from Glasgow and from Carlisle. The obvious remedy was to double this stretch; the track formation and overbridges allowed for it. They quickly doubled the section Dunragit–Castle Kennedy and then, for some reason which I could never fathom, stopped. So, for all the war period, a train coming from the Carlisle direction had continuous track circuiting from Glenluce to Dunragit, double line block to Castle Kennedy, tablet to Cairnryan Junction, tablet to the Harbour Junction, and tablet to the Harbour – rather an obstacle race.

On 3 June 1942, King George VI and Queen Elizabeth paid a visit to Scotland, travelling during the night. They had a train of 440 tons and hauled by two Kingmoor compounds, Nos 1141 and 1145. They passed New Cumnock about 3.00am, and some genius arranged to put them down the Catrine branch for the remainder of the night. A Caley Class 3F 0–6–0 was put at the rear end to supply steam heat. At a suitable hour of morning they set off again. Now the Catrine branch consisted of $1\frac{1}{4}$ miles of 1 in 60 right up to the junction, with a final sharp curve. The rail was probably wet, the compounds slipped furiously, and they came to a dead stand three times. Finally they had to get the steam-heat engine up to push in the rear. They got to Kilmarnock, and there discovered that in the struggles No 1141 had broken a spring hanger. Corkerhill was standing by with a spare compound, No 913 with driver James McCreadie, which was dispatched at once. Tender-first they went on the Canal line, round by Muirhouse and Strathbungo Junction on to the Barrhead road, and 40 minutes from the receipt of the call, nearly blinded by coal-dust, they delivered No 913 at Kilmarnock.

Jimmy McCreadie – what a splendid man he was – always neat and tidy, always cheerful, always ready to do the best he could. He belonged about Dailly, I think, but he seemed to have friends in every port down Stranraer way. In the time of severe rationing, they would be up at each station with a dozen eggs or a pound of butter or a pair of rabbits. When he was on the 4.20pm from Stranraer the toolbox would be like a provision store!

About three weeks after the Catrine episode their Majesties paid a visit to Northern Ireland, and it was arranged that they would travel via the Cairnryan Military Railway and the new port. The full Royal Train did not go down the CMR; a two-coach train was provided, the Caley officers' saloon and a newly-decorated first brake. Stranraer got out its best Class 2P 4–4–0 No 600, and they cleaned, scrubbed and polished to perfection. Willie Dunlop and Bob Collins were the two that were to man No 600, and shortly before zero hour Willie Dunlop came to foreman Martin. 'There's something serious wrong with that engine,' he reported. A hurried examination revealed tubes gone; they were running like a burn! 'Listen,' said Martin, 'there's no time to polish up another engine. Get them to Cairnryan, if we have to carry you back!' They very nearly had to do that, but they got their Majesties safely to Deep Water Wharf. Two days later, on 26 June 1942, the Royal Party returned. No 600 was still out for the count; they had to borrow another class 2P from Dumfries, No 614. This proved if anything rather worse than No 600. However, Stranraer men George ('Munch') Harvey and Hugh Dalrymple managed to keep going till they got to the temporary platform at the junction, where the passengers transferred to the main line Royal Train.

I mentioned the 4.20pm from Stranraer Town station to Glasgow. Its schedule as far as Girvan was one of the freaks of wartime. By 1941 most trains had had their schedules eased to a considerable extent, but that of the 4.20pm had gone in the opposite direction. In the final peace timetable of 1939, this train had an allowance of 77 minutes for the 37.3 miles to Girvan, with seven stops. The wartime schedule was 71 minutes. This was a very hard job, with anything of a load. Corkerhill men worked it; they ran the 12.30pm to Stranraer and the 4.20pm back, getting a fresh engine from Stranraer. Running times totalled 67 minutes. I timed ten runs on this train in 1940–2; on only three of them was this running time exceeded, and that by seconds only. There were some grand engines about that time. I came on the footplate of the 4.20pm on 17 August 1940; No 5731 was the engine, with Jimmy Murray (him they called 'Dungaree'), and Joe Byers firing. We had seven coaches, 211 tons, and they were full. It is strange to look back on that journey. Our country was in direst peril, yet there we were on that glorious day of sunshine, that splendid engine roaring up those hills – 45 per cent cut-off and full regulator, and we were still going more than 30mph at the head of the Swan's Neck. And there was old Dungaree, hammering on, and yarning happily of his boyhood days in Dalbeattie, and every time I went over to the fireman's side I got another grump from Joe about the way The Dungaree was hitting her! 60 minutes 7 seconds, that was our running time to Girvan. It was amazing to think that not long before, the LMS authorities had required years of urging and a test run before they would reduce the non-stop schedule of the Paddy from 72 to 66 minutes!

Stranraer men had some heavy work, too. They ran to Glasgow with the 11.55am, returning on the 5.10pm, still non-stop to Ayr. Its schedule had been eased from 45 minutes to 51 minutes, but in place of a nice train of eight coaches there were 14, often full and with passengers standing. Four coaches came off at Ayr and two more at Girvan, but the engine still had to tackle Glendoune with eight. But the engines were good – usually a Class 5X from Kingmoor or Crewe North. When Sandy McKnight and Harry Anderson were on that job, they used to carry an extra shovel, then when it came to a bit of heavy work, it was one on each side of the firebox to shovel in coal. One night they were on the first portion of the London Paddy (10.00pm ex-Stranraer Harbour). They had a Crewe Class 5X, a good one, and a load of 305 tons, just nice for the Port Road, with its ruling grade of 1 in 80. Just before the start came word of a derailment at Southwick and everything to be diverted via Girvan, Ayr, and Mauchline. This was quite a different problem, for with their 305 tons they had to tackle New Luce bank, with its three miles of 1 in 57. 'Oh Sanny, we canna gie ye a pilot! There's no' an engine aboot the place. Ye'll jist hae tae gae on an' dae the best ye can.' They did even that; they went through New Luce full tilt and up the bank as best they could; but she just went up to about a mile from the top and came to a stand in full forward gear and full regulator! They were 57 minutes on The Neck dividing the train, and it was 4.00am before they got to Carlisle. Likewise it was midday before they got back, as passengers, to Stranraer.

In May 1941 there came to Ayr an evacuee from Southern England, Southern Railway No 2605, none other than a D1 0–4–2T of Stroudley's LBSCR design, and one of the oldest of the class at that. It was in malachite green, and when put on as shunter at Ayr passenger station was the cynosure of all eyes. Several of the elderly drivers had it on that job, Jimmy Cairns the longest, and they kept it beautifully clean. She was a fine, handy wee engine, but going bunker-first into a siding with a sharp turnout she simply slammed her tail over – I was nearly put out of the door the first time I was on her.

On 15 November 1941 the 12.30pm from Glasgow to Stranraer was loaded to 328 tons, all going through. Garry Teirl had a Class 5X, not doing too well. Ayr did not have a spare engine to assist, so they attached No 2605, and it piloted them to Girvan. At a later date the 12.30pm was again in distress. Archie Davie with No 5565 with a bad blow from the superheater header. Davie Graham, an Ayr man from the Class 2P link, was on the pilot with No 2605. They put him on in front. No assistance was available at Girvan, so they topped up No 2605's tank and went on south. Archie Davie let them off at Glenwhilly, and they made their way back light engine. No 2605 must have seemed a queer wee fragment of green scuttling back alone over those vast brown moors.

Ayr had another D1 0–4–2T, SR No 2284. It was a sad contrast to 2605, being extremely grimy and in poor order, and so was kept discreetly in the background, mostly on goods yard work round Ayr. It proved useful, however, as a substitute for the diesel shunter at Grangeston munition factory, $1\frac{1}{4}$ miles north of Girvan, which shunter had a habit of breaking down.

A two-platform halt was erected at Grangeston, and two workers' trains ran to it from Ayr each morning. These trains went on to Girvan station, reversing there and going to Turnberry where, as in the first world war, the famous golf courses were being converted to an aerodrome. Two similar trains worked back in the evening.

On 29 April 1942, my friend Tommy Hopes, having escaped from Singapore the night before the city fell to the Japanese, travelled home to Dalmellington in the 6.20pm ex-Ayr, driven by Anthony Ross on No 664. It was no peaceful home-coming, for regular troops stationed in Ayrshire were staging an attack upon the town of Dalmellington, whose Home Guard was putting up a vigorous resistance. They tell me it was quite a show, and old Tony Ross was so fascinated by the spectacle that he failed to observe that the gates at Sillyhole crossing were across the line. He crashed through them which, of course, is not done in the best circles.

Tommy Gibson, shunter at Ayr, went in 1939 to Kilmarnock as passenger guard. To get a house there proved impossible; he travelled to and from his home in Ayr as shifts permitted. One Saturday shift was difficult; the Glasgow–New Cumnock train was then extended to Sanquhar. To get back with the empty coaches to Kilmarnock and let Tommy get the last train for Ayr was mighty tight work, but the engine crew said they would do it. They cut out turning at New Cumnock. Tender first all the way they tore at it, shot out of Mossgiel Tunnel and away for a hurricane descent on Kilmarnock when on went the brakes. Tommy fell off his seat and slid along the floor of the van. He picked himself up and looked out, to see a red lamp being waved vigorously from Garrochburn box. Word had come from Hurlford that an up goods had passed, and in the blackout the signalman had thought he saw something protruding and probably fouling the down line. The Garrochburn man kept his up signals on, and presently the goods whistled and drew slowly up to the home. Tommy made his way down the line, told the goods enginemen and proceeded to inspect the train. There it was, an army tank, its gun turret slewed round and the gun projecting over the down line! Tommy went on to tell the goods guard. He found him, a poor old superannuated man, brought back to service in wartime, fast asleep with his boots off! He was useless, so Tommy and the other men got up on the tank and tried to find how the turret worked (in the blackout.) It was locked solid; the only course open was to detach the vehicle. At Garrochburn there was only a very small yard for farm traffic, its sleepers probably not renewed for many many years. On the up side was a siding for coal traffic from Mauchline Colliery, its track probably equally rickety. They chose the down yard. One can imagine the anxiety as that ponderous vehicle was shunted, inch by inch, over that yielding track. They got it in. They must have been sweating big drops!

Tommy had a problem of a different sort another evening in wartime. He was on a train from Ardrossan to Kilmarnock, with its normal make-up of two coaches – one, providentially, was a Caley 12-wheeled non-corridor composite. At South Beach there was waiting a party of 350 for Springside. At Irvine was the usual crowd from the dog-racing track. They did not leave anyone! Will Neilson of Hurlford was the driver ('Kilmaurs Will'). There were five railwaymen among the passengers and Neilson took those on to the engine. The rest they packed in. When they left Irvine, Tommy got his legs inside the van; as far as Springside he had to lean out of the window. I think the end compartment of those 12-wheelers was a little larger than the rest; in it were counted 26 persons, the adults on the seats and floor, the children in the racks! There were also two greyhounds. When they discharged the Springside contingent Tommy said you could see the sides of the coaches falling back into place! How we could welcome their spirit on a snowy night when a busy bus sails past and leaves us at a stop!

9

Feeling the Strain

Girvan has two signal boxes; No 1 controls the junction for the branch to the goods yard and locomotive depot; No 2 is at the passenger station. Wartime traffic used to produce a few headaches for the nightshift signalman in No 2 box.

The 11.35pm goods from College arrived at Girvan around 3.30am. If they had anything for the goods yard the locomotive crew would take water on the branch and so come up through the passenger station non-stop and charge Glendoune bank, not that there was much way on by the time the train was past the hospital. The section was right through to Pinwherry at that time of morning and that would take the most of 60 minutes; with a bad rail or a bad engine they might take 80 or 90 minutes. Meanwhile, the 1.00am from College had arrived and was waiting to go up, probably taking water at the up platform. Somewhere up the line both those trains would have to cross the 'Big Cairriages' – the empty stock of the Cardiff leave train – 15 or 16 coaches.

The workers' train from Bargany colliery came next and had to be quickly shunted for the two workers' trains from Ayr to Grangeston. Both had to reverse in the station and go on to Turnberry. One of the engines had to get precedence, as it took a morning passenger to Ayr. Close on their heels came the 5.00am goods from Falkland Junction to Stranraer. This would usually take water at the station and then go on to cross with a goods from Stranraer and an exchange of crews. If by this time there was breathing space the Big Cairriages were brought down at last with their two weary old River 4–6–0s – Ayr men called them the *Scharnhorst* and the *Gneisenau*. Both would be gasping for water, so that meant blocking the whole station for at least 20 minutes. By the time they had cleared, the Stranraer–Glasgow milk had to be got down. If this was in good time, it would be allowed to run ahead of the 7.20am passenger ex-Stranraer, but usually it would be shunted, sometimes to the station sidings, sometimes to the goods branch. One morning a young Stranraer man was rather too enthusiastic in shunting into the sidings and put 1,500 gallons of milk over the buffers and into Bourtreehall.

On 27 February 1942 I visited Girvan No 2 box and noted from the register the up trains they had dealt with that day. I had no time to record the down trains, but the list is of interest:

Train	Locomotive No.	Class
11.35pm College–Stranraer goods	14636	Caley 60 4–6–0
1.00am College–Stranraer goods	5645	LMS 5X 4–6–0
6.30am Bargany workers	598	LMS 2P 4–4–0
6.48am Ayr–Turnberry workers	590	LMS 2P 4–4–0
7.00am Ayr–Turnberry workers	592	LMS 2P 4–4–0
5.00am Ayr–Stranraer goods	17262 2880	Caley 2F 0–6–0 LMS Mogul 2–6–0
7.04am Glasgow–Girvan passenger	571	LMS 2P 4–4–0
9.40am Girvan–Stranraer goods	5566	LMS 5X 4–6–0
10.15am Turnberry–Girvan passenger	592	LMS 2P 4–4–0
8.55am Glasgow–Stranraer passenger	5053	LMS 5P 4–6–0
10.45am Glasgow–Girvan passenger	576	LMS 2P 4–4–0
12.30pm Glasgow–Stranraer passenger	5575	LMS 5X 4–6–0
Empty coaches of leave train	14760 14758	Highland 4–6–0 Highland 4–6–0
1.00pm Girvan–Stranraer goods	5690	LMS 5X 4–6–0
2.20pm Glasgow–Girvan passenger	664	LMS 2P 4–4–0
4.15pm Glasgow–Girvan passenger	1136	LMS Compound 4–4–0
5.10pm Glasgow–Stranraer passenger	5578	LMS 5X 4–6–0
Milk empties, Glasgow–Stranraer (The milk empties comprised 19 vans, 442 tons).	598 14651	LMS 2P 4–4–0 Caley 60 4–6–0

That was routine stuff; there were also emergencies. Johnnie Walker was on night shift and the 1.00am from Glasgow was approaching the station when the telephone rang. Pinwherry . . . 'Try an' stop the 1.00am, that's the "Obstruction" from Barrhill!' By this time the engine was past the box and the starting signal. Johnnie flung back the lever of his advance starter. The driver saw it, shut-off and came to a stop. Then apparently he thought it was just a mistake, so he picked-up and went on, with Johnnie trying in vain to attract the attention of the guard. Back to the telephone. The 1.45am goods ex-Stranraer, which normally stopped for water at Barrhill, had run past, obviously out of control. If it could not stop at Barrhill, there was even less chance of its stopping at Pinwherry — it would go right through into the Girvan section and meet the 1.00am head-on! There ensued 20 minutes of acute anxiety for three signalmen, then there came word from Barrhill that the Stranraer men had got a grip of their train further down the hill, and had propelled back to Barrhill station. That was perhaps exceptional; there was always the worry of a Greyback going away up Glendoune, failing to make it, and coming back, usually when the station was full and with no free lines.

Oh, those Greybacks — what a time they had with them! I was really sorry about them. I had thought that after all those years of condemnation and poor performance, they had found on the G&SW section men who had got the secret of working them and who were on the way to real success. Then came the war, and with the conditions of working and maintenance all hope of improvement went by the board. Braking ability was one of the chief problems. The Corkerhill engines were largely engaged in working non-fitted goods trains over the Stranraer line. For such working, an essential was a good engine brake. The Greybacks had only the Westinghouse, no longer required for working passenger trains, and certainly not a first priority for maintenance. They also had a vacuum ejector and trainpipes, and after some near-runaways it was laid down that a Greyback working with anything near full load over the Stranraer road had to have at least five vacuum-fitted vehicles next to the engine.

Above: LMS Horwich 2-6-0 No 2807 near head of Glendoune Bank.
F. R. Hebron

Below: Glasgow–Stranraer Harbour train at Girvan. LMS 4-4-0 compound
No 910 and Horwich 2-6-0.
W. Tennant

Above: Glenwhilly station.
H. D. Bowtell

Below: Holehouse Junction under snow, January 1940.
D. L. Smith collection

Steaming seemed to be a constant worry. The Greybacks did not appear to have been brilliant at any time, and with unskilled firemen and the deterioration in the quality of coal in wartime, matters got very bad.

Two or my friends at Corkerhill told me of their experiences with those engines. Davie Wightman was on the Stranraer run in the autumn of 1942. On the 6.15pm ex-Stranraer he had No 14636, reputedly a 'weak one', with 29 wagons. He put her at New Luce bank as hard as she would go, but with full open regulator and full forward gear the engine came to a stand at Milepost 23. They divided the train, and by the time they got the second portion up to Glenwhilly the tender tank was dry and they could not even run to Barrhill! On his next trip he had No 14638 and full load. The engine slipped about Wilson's Hoose, so he put her into full forward gear and gave her just what regulator she would stand, and they got up all right.

About the same period Jimmy Copeland was on that train. He had only a young passed cleaner with him. They had had a Class 5X on the way to Stranraer, and had had a quite good trip. When they came out for the 6.15pm, here was a Greyback waiting for them. The boy nearly fainted! 'Now, now,' said Jimmy, 'don't be getting excited. I've had a fair experience of these engines. You do as I tell you and we'll get on not so bad.' So he made up the fire himself, then he turned to the water-gauge and put his finger on the half-way position. 'Now,' he said to the fireman, 'keep your water-level *there*. Don't let her rise any higher.' They got away, and the boy obeyed orders and kept the water at half-glass. The boiler pressure rose and presently the washout plugs began to fizz. The fireman got ready to jump over the side! 'Don't worry,' said Jimmy, 'they do that when you work them at half-glass. The Manson six-couplers were the same. There's nothing wrong.' 'We had a grand trip,' he told me, 'plenty of steam all the way, and she pulled like a good one.'

I am afraid that few trips worked out so well as that one. I heard grisly tales of the other kind. Then in addition there were mechanical breakdowns. One day in February 1941, Greyback

No 14644 was on the 1.00pm goods from Girvan to Stranraer. A ballast train was going south also, so Control ordered the two to be combined. They went up Glendoune and No 14644 broke a valve, so the whole outfit had to come back down to Girvan, and the goods was cancelled.

On 24 April 1942 Norrie Robertson of Corkerhill was on the 5.00pm Stranraer–Glasgow goods with No 14630. As he came out of Pinmore tunnel he shut off steam. The nut came off the end of the left-hand piston rod. The piston head came free and knocked off the cylinder-cover. The cover brought about half of the cylinder barrel with it. Fortunately the broken parts fell clear and went down the banking. All else remained intact, and Robertson was able to make his way slowly down to Girvan. He could not, however, put his train back into Girvan Goods, so Willie Candlish of Ayr, with a class 2P 4–4–0, helped him in. After that, Candlish was sent up to the tunnel to retrieve the broken bits, only to discover that those were too heavy for him and his fireman to lift. They returned to Girvan, picked up No 14630's goods train and worked it forward to Ayr. No 14651 came down next day and towed No 14630 away to the works.

They also put the Greybacks on passenger work, even on the hard-booked 4.20pm. I timed only one run on that train behind Greyback, No 14630, 13 December 1941, with Jock Mulholland and Bobby Dodds, and a rather moderate load of 149 tons to Girvan and 244 tons thereafter. We got to Girvan in a running time of 67 minutes 34 seconds (67 booked), but after that I could sense that they were getting short of steam. Archie Davie had a worse job, on 31 July 1942. He had No 14633 with seven coaches from Stranraer and eleven from Girvan. He told me he had the regulator full open and full forward gear up New Luce bank and Killochan bank. He was 40 minutes late at Ayr.

By then the coal was getting very bad. I always remember the night of 2 October 1942. I went up to Ayr station, to be told that the 4.20pm was in distress, and was coming coupled to a 'special'. Due in Ayr at 6.10pm, they pulled in at 7.57pm, Tam Young of Ayr with No 656 piloting No 14637 with Jimmy Tweedie and

Jimmy Balmer, Bob's son. On the rear of the train was an officers' saloon. Tweedie got off and tottered wearily past me to wind the lubricator. He was a sight. He had lost his cap, he was powdered from head to foot with white ash, and he had a thick streak of black oil down one cheek. Jimmy Balmer jumped up to fill the tank, and I called to him that I would put some coal in her. I dived beneath the anti-glare sheet and yanked the firedoor open, whereupon a quantity of the fire fell out on to the footplate. By the time I got that back in I was confronted by a wall of what looked like faintly incandescent cement. I had to dig a hole in this before I could get some fresh coal in. They told me that they had had an awful time. She would not steam right from the start. They sat for a long time at Dunragit blowing-up, then they got on to New Luce. There they sat 15 minutes blowing and blowing but the boiler pressure never rose a pound. They had four coaches and three vans on, but they tackled the bank. They kept the injector on all the way up, but got to Glenwhilly with the water out of sight. An officers' special was following, so it was brought up to Glenwhilly, the saloon attached in rear, and No 656 attached in front. There was no improvement, but the Class 2P kept them going. From Girvan they had eight coaches and the three vans. At Ayr Jock McCusker of Corkerhill relieved Tam Young and No 656 went on to Glasgow with them. By 1943 the authorities had realised that Greybacks on the Stranraer line were more a liability than an asset, and all were removed from Corkerhill.

With bad coal and lack of maintenance it was not only the Greybacks that were in trouble. On 30 July 1942, Archie Davie was on the 4.20pm with No 5575 and seven coaches. He got to Glenwhilly and to his surprise another Class 5X backed on to pilot him. It turned out that the other man's tank was dry, so Archie pulled the train and pushed him until they got to Barrhill! On 21 August 1942 Mulholland had No 5575 on the 4.20pm with Inspector Willie Still on the footplate. The train was very heavy, 263 tons from Stranraer and 386 from Girvan and even Still, a man of much experience on the Caley, could not make the engine steam. They were 44 minutes late at Pinwherry. At Girvan, old

Tony Ross was in with his Class 2P No 664, so this was coupled on in front, tender-first, and he piloted them to Ayr, reached 53 minutes late. Tommy Coffield had a similar experience with No 5644. He had seven coaches and two vans from Stranraer, with three more added at Girvan. They were almost beaten on the Swan's Neck. They telephoned Girvan for assistance, but had to wait there for 15 minutes till they got an Ayr Class 2P with Bob Cleary to pilot them through to Glasgow.

I do not want to give the impression that the 5Xs, as a class, were poor steamers, not at all. But the Class 5Xs at Corkerhill were rather a poor lot. They were not in good condition when they came, and Northern Division maintenance did not appear to make them any better. One curious experience – I saw No 5645 go through Kilkerran at 66mph and come to a dead stand in the Marl Hole, $3\frac{1}{4}$ miles further on, with 130lb/sq in boiler pressure showing, the vacuum down to 13in, and the water out of sight.

The Corkerhill top link also had the running of the 10.00am London express as far as Carlisle, returning on the 10.30am from Leeds. The engines were usually from Holbeck, and in splendid condition. In August 1942 I had two trips on the 10.00am, and both were of high quality. In each case a Class 2P from Hurlford piloted from St Enoch to New Cumnock, Archie Davie and Danny Broom had No 5597, with 382 tons to Dumfries and 435 tons beyond. Jock Mulholland and Ian Middleton had No 5604, with 375 tons throughout. I quote those tonnages, but actually they bear little resemblance to the tonnage to be hauled. On the first trip I was going through to Leeds, and in view of my limited 'standing' ability, I booked first-class and just got a seat at Kilmarnock. On the second, I was going to Carlisle only, so travelled third-class, as it was then. I was lucky. I stood opposite the end table in an open vestibule coach and I could lean on the edge of the table. From my position I made a count. Sitting and standing, there were 75 people in that coach, excluding those in the cross-passages at the ends, which I knew were packed solid. Most passengers would have luggage, heavy luggage in the case of servicemen. It made the tare weight of your train look a bit sick.

Two months later, Archie Davie and Danny Broom were again on the 10.00am turn. They were going in light engine from Corkerhill to St Enoch, with a number of enginemen on the footplate — men going to relieve shunting pilots, and so on, and Danny Broom was standing back at the tender bulkhead. The engine was coaled high for through working to Leeds; Bellahouston footbridge combed a big lump off the top; it struck Danny on the head and killed him.

Through working of the Corkerhill enginemen to England had ceased at the outbreak of war. To my surprise it was revived about the beginning of 1943. It was asking a lot of men to learn 113 miles of road in wartime and blackout; one wondered where the advantage lay. None of the old Leeds link remained; the four chosen, Archie Davie, Garry Teirl, Jimmy Tweedie and Tommy Coffield had all to learn from scratch.

There was one comfort; as I have said, they would be getting better engines. New and exciting varieties were appearing. Already Mulholland was telling me of a splendid run he had had on the 6.40pm from Carlisle with No 5736, one of the two Class 5X engines rebuilt with the bigger boiler and double chimney. Then on the 1.55pm ex-Carlisle Tweedie had none other than No 6170 *British Legion* the unique Royal Scot with taper boiler which had been rebuilt out of the experimental *Fury*. His load was made up at Dumfries to 450 tons, and No 6170 took that to Glasgow in splendid fashion. Then the rebuilt Scots with new taper boilers came out — No 6109 was one of the first. On 20 August 1943 Archie Davie had it on the 3.50pm to Leeds. The locomotive had a speedometer, and going through Cummertrees Archie had just noticed with interest that they were doing 80mph, when it lurched and nearly broke his jaw on the window-frame!

One of the most exciting turns for the Corkerhill boys was the 4.53am newspaper train to Kilmarnock and forward by the 6.06am local to Dumfries. There they remanned the 7.15am local from Carlisle, a bit of a freak, for on a train of six or seven coaches there was a Duchess 4—6—2, some of which were still streamlined. Time could be made up easily, despite twelve stops to Kilmarnock. One morning in January 1943 young Hughie Ritchie was deputising for Jimmy McCreadie. He got No 6228, left Dumfries at 9.00am, 30 minutes late, and was in St Enoch on time, 10.57am.

It may be noticed that there are few references to breakaways in wartime. This I attribute to the eradication of double-heading over those difficult grades, and the substitution of more trains, single-headed. I have a note of a breakaway south of Pinmore on 22 July 1941, with the 1.00am, still double-headed, and there was one on 16 October 1941 at a rather unusual place. A train of 45 wagons of ashes was being worked down from Glasgow for the ballasting of the Cairnryan line. It was hauled by a compound and a Greyback. They came over the North Johnstone road and broke away somewhere about Kilbirnie. The two portions came together just at Swinlees, the landscape was decorated in ashes, and a signal gantry was knocked down.

On 17 January 1944 there occurred the only breakaway in which I was ever involved personally. There was some information that I wanted, so I went up to Ayr station to contact the men on the 5.15pm ex-Glasgow. The main up platform was extremely dark. I encountered the old carriage examiner and stood chatting with him. Presently a down goods came through, with No 574 and three goods vehicles. I was slowly pondering whether Ayr had been added to the list of places where short goods trains can be run without a brake van when the old examiner went off like a rocket, 'Hey, hey! There's a man away wi' half his train! Stop him! Stop him!' and off he galloped for the footbridge. I had always been told that in the case of a breakaway the main consideration was to keep the first portion going, and as speedily as possible, and here they were going to stop it. I could not help that. The next was to get word to the guard, who was probably unaware of the mishap. But where was the second portion, was it coming on, and at what speed? There was not a railway employee to be seen. I moved up to the big overbridge and listened, and just then the 5.15pm ran in, with No 5644 blowing-off steam fit to bring the house down, and blotting out all view of the down line. I reached the overbridge, and was groping my way down the ramp towards platform 6 when a shadow, darker than the darkness under the bridge, loomed up, a big oil tank wagon. It was coming steadily, maybe about 10mph, fast enough to cause a considerable spill. Behind was a considerable train, but just as I neared platform 6 I glimpsed the side lights of the brake van. I rushed up to platform 6 only to discover it full to the buffers with a train between me and the line with the runaway. I climbed on to the buffer stops, got out to the end – the van was coming nearer. I thought that I could just distinguish the figure of the guard, leaning out of his end door. 'Broke away!' I yelled. I thought I saw him lean towards me. 'You're broke away!!' I yelled again. The figure vanished, there was a sudden clatter of boots, then 'eek-eek-eek' went the brake, and I could hear the snatch of couplings. I could do no more; I scrambled down, made my way back to the station. I was just under the bridge when I heard the clash, then a wild crescendo of banging buffers, culminating in a grand slam just at my ear. I got on to the platform and over the footbridge. The crash had occurred within the station – they had been bringing the front part back!! However, nothing had been damaged. The guard was retailing his experience to an eager circle of listeners. 'The couplin's no' broken,' he reported. 'We were stopped back at Belmont. It must have jumped off the hook then. I didna ken onything aboot it till Big Will McQuiston came doon frae the Cattle Market and cried tae me that we were broke away.' I slipped modestly away into the surrounding darkness. Now I know what I looked like in the blackout.

Dumfries was a station which handled a tremendous traffic in wartime. I marvelled as I saw a train from Kirkcudbright to the Midland Division on 8 July 1944. There were a van, three corridors, a match truck, ten well-wagons each with a tank, a match truck, and a corridor composite. The tare weight would be about 670 tons. It went out of Carlisle with Mogul No 2764, and Stanier 2–8–0 No 8138. Dumfries shed, once full of Class 2P 4–4–0s and Caley class 2F 0–6–0s, was gradually changing. A Royal Scot could usually be seen, probably in from Kingmoor. Compounds were accumulating, some well-known, like Nos 1135 and 1144 from Kingmoor, Nos 902 and 904 from Polmadie, No 912 and dear old No 1179 from Corkerhill. The Kirkcudbright engine was now No 170, a Stanier 2–6–2T. For the line to Lockerbie they had sent down a L&NW push-and-pull outfit, with a Webb 2–4–2 tank. Besides its Lockerbie activities, the push-and-pull did at least one turn on the main line. I noted No 6639 on it several times.

The little push-and-pull was involved in a tragic accident which took place at Dumfries passenger station on the fine summer evening of 12 June 1944. Dumfries No 1 signalbox stood a little distance north of the passenger station, on the down side. It controlled the junctions to Stranraer (west) and Lockerbie (east). Dumfries No 2 was south of the station, on the down side opposite the locomotive yard. The down distant for Dumfries No 1 was slotted with the down starter for No 2. On that evening an empty carriage train was being worked down the G&SW line. It was M950, the 1.50pm from Waterloo Sidings, Leeds, to Woodhill, Kilmarnock. It consisted of ten corridors, and was hauled by Class 5X No 5660. It stopped at Kingmoor and was there re-manned by Driver H. Harkness and Fireman J. Barnes, both of Kingmoor. It left Kingmoor at 8.48pm. The signalman at Dumfries No 1 knew of the approach of this empty carriage train. He concluded that, as was usual with such trains, it would take water at Dumfries from the column at the north end of the down platform. He had two trains under his care just then, the 5.00pm goods from Stranraer to Carlisle, and the push-and-pull, which was to form the 9.50pm workers' to Powfoot, a halt west of Annan, serving a wartime munitions factory. The Stranraer train was coming on the up Stranraer line; it had to be crossed-over the down main line to the up main and so south. The push-and-pull was sitting at the box on the down Stranraer line. As soon as the goods was past, it would go through the crossover and over to the up main platform. The engine was at the Stranraer end of the set, with the fireman on the footplate. Driver James Kenning, of Dumfries, was in the driving compartment at the Dumfries end.

No 2 box offered the down empty carriage train to No 1, whose signalman accepted under Regulation 4 'line clear to down starter.' He kept his home and distant on, then he gave the road to the up Stranraer goods. To do this, he had to set his junction for the down Stranraer line also. What he did not know was that his down distant arm was not on as he thought, but *off*. It was slotted with No 2 starter, the slot had stuck, and when No 2 pulled off his starter, No 1's distant came off with it. When this happened, No 2 pulled off his distant, and so did Nos 3 and 4. No 1 man did not observe this incorrect aspect on his repeater, although about 4.20pm that afternoon the driver of a down goods had been misled with it, and had shouted to the signalman that his distant was showing clear. The signalman could not, however, hear him.

What precipitated disaster was that the driver of the empty carriages had no intention of stopping for water. With all four distants off, he came sweeping along about 40mph, to be confronted by No 1 home *on*. Having little warning, he apparently made a full brake application, then they swerved on to the Stranraer line. Right in front of them was the push-pull; he and the fireman both jumped from the left-hand side. They hit coaches standing on an adjacent line, fell back under their own train, and were both killed.

The elderly driver of the push-pull suddenly saw the class 5X coming head-on towards him. He tried to open the door and jump, but did not succeed. No 5660 smashed in the end of the compartment and went right inside the vehicle. The old man was badly hurt and shocked, and died in hospital the following morning. It was a pitiful business, for when the breakdown gang got in to the footplate of the Class 5X, they found that the shovel had not slid out of the coal-pile, and the tea-jars were still sitting on the shelf above the firedoor.

Tragic, tragic − yet the work had to go on, and what work it was! I did not, of course, see much of the main line, but on two wartime visits to Carlisle, my friends in Carlisle Control told me incredible things. Carlisle was still its old, tangled, pre-Grouping layout, with seven goods yards of the old companies − no huge, modern Kingmoor marshalling yard. They told me of yards choked with traffic, of a freight train in every block section for 50 miles back. 'Shunt your train and come in engine and van.' They told me of the Goods Lines, trains nose-to-tail, unable to move owing to congestion in the yards ahead. They would relieve men whose day was up; eight hours later they would relieve the relief crew, the train still at the same spot. There were maddening difficulties – a train all made up and manned, but no brake van available in the whole of Carlisle, a train all ready to go but no shovel on the engine. But they got the traffic through somehow, a saga that may never be told.

It was scarcely so hectic on the Ayr road. My notes of happenings in this last year of the war are again rather scanty. On the whole things seemed to improve, and engines were in better condition than in the difficult days of 1942/3. All honour to the fitters who kept them so. The Class 5Xs still pounded up hill and down dale, with now a good admixture of Class 5s and Moguls to assist. Class 2P ran most of the Glasgow traffic; Caley 2F and 3F handled the freight. There are notes of odd little incidents – War Department 2–10–0 No 3730 visiting Ayr on a ballast, of all things, two of our commonplace Hurlford Class 2Ps, Nos 688 and 661, on a 13-coach train of American troops, an army truck with four French paratroopers falling on the line from Patna station bridge just in front of the 6.20pm Dalmellington. Claudie Cumming could have had only 100yd view of them as he came through Dalharco bridge, but he managed to stop, which was good work. A queer little item that impressed me was the clatter of feet down King Street, Castle Douglas, at midnight – the late-shift munition workers coming off their train.

In the early summer of 1945 the war ended. I can remember no particular rejoicing – the men did not deck out their engines in bunting or anything like that, there was little reference in conversation. I think we were all a bit tired. And at home I extricated from their various hiding-places my diaries and notebooks, secreted since the start of the war in case of a German invasion. It is very strange to look at them now and remember those things.

10

The Longest Section

After the war, in the period 1946/7, there occurred two incidents concerning which I was able to obtain particulars in much fuller detail than usual. Those details I have set down in this and the succeeding chapter.

The scene of the first incident was that very long section of single line between Barrhill and Glenwhilly, $8\frac{1}{2}$ miles, the longest distance between two block posts on the old G&SW. From Barrhill station (milepost $12\frac{1}{2}$) the line climbs steeply to the summit at milepost $16\frac{1}{2}$, then descends by gentler gradients to Glenwhilly station (milepost 21). The country is almost entirely bleak moorland; for the first $6\frac{3}{4}$ miles from Barrhill there is no habitation in sight, save for a brief glimpse of the farm of Chirmorie, a mile away to the east. This farm gives its name to the summit point, but there has never been a station or signalbox at the summit. At $19\frac{1}{4}$ miles, the farm of Miltonish is seen to the east of the line, with the smaller farm of Markdow on the hill to the west. A mile further on is the farm of Marklach, (west side) then Glenwhilly farm (east) about a $\frac{1}{2}$-mile from the station. Glenwhilly has a crossing-loop, two platforms, signalbox and station house on the up platform, with some four railwaymen's houses adjacent.

A road runs from Barrhill station to the village of New Luce, passing near to Glenwhilly station. It is still narrow and twisting, but at the time of this incident it was poorly surfaced, rutted and partly grass-grown; there were a number of gates across it. For a mile from Barrhill station this road keeps near to the railway on the east side, then it swings away to the east and is out of sight of the railway for $5\frac{1}{2}$ miles till it returns at Miltonish farm, and is to the east of the line to Glenwhilly.

137

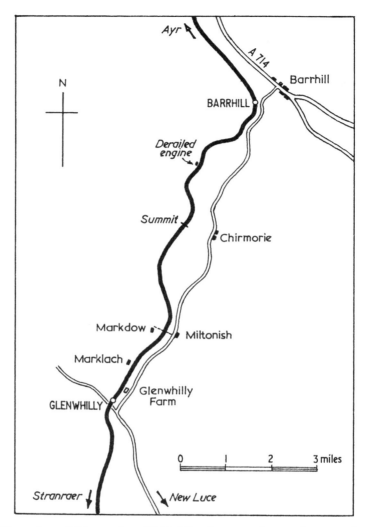

Saturday, 2 November 1946. The day was fine and sunny, but there was a raw, cold air, and a thick drizzle set in at dusk. It was a big day for Stranraer, for their football team was playing Edinburgh City at Ayr in the South Section Qualifying Cup Final, and a nine-coach special, packed to the roofs, had left for Ayr in the forenoon, taking all from Stranraer locomotive and traffic departments who could possibly get away.

Trouble began about 1.00pm, when the locomotive of the 1.00pm freight from Girvan to Stranraer, running early, failed at Pinmore with both injectors out of action. This was Class 5 4–6–0 No 5490, with a train of 17 wagons and van. Its driver, William Kilpatrick, of Stranraer, notified Stranraer motive power depot, and a relief engine was prepared and dispatched, Class 5X No 5676 *Codrington*, belonging to Crewe North. The crew consisted of passed fireman Hugh Dalrymple, on his thirteenth driving turn, and cleaner William Allison, on his first firing turn. Tender-first, they left Stranraer at 1.40pm, and running very moderately reached Glenwhilly at 2.18pm. Two minutes later they entered the long section across the moors to Barrhill.

About its booked time of 2.27pm, the 12.30pm passenger train from Glasgow arrived at Barrhill, hauled by Class 5X No 5645 with driver William Scott ('The Big Min') and fireman George Stratton, both of Corkerhill. They were held at Barrhill, being informed that a light engine from Glenwhilly was in the section. They waited and waited, but no sound came from the silent moor, so after much discussion Stratton volunteered to go forward on foot, and at 2.55pm he disappeared into the wilderness. Another hour went by, but no sign of him. Stationmaster Gilbert Clark got fairly worried and dispatched porter–signalman Jackie Griffin to try his luck, but just round the first curve Griffin met Stratton returning. Stratton reported that he had found the light engine, derailed near milepost $14\frac{1}{2}$, two miles out.

It appears that *Codrington* and its juvenile crew were descending from Chirmorie summit when running became alarmingly rough, and eventually they applied the brake and stopped, to discover that two pairs of coupled wheels were off the road, though bogie and tender wheels were still on. Dalrymple was presented with the problem of a lifetime. Here he was, his big heavy engine derailed on a single line in desolate country and a completely inexperienced fireman. The boy would need to walk to the end of the section with the tablet, summon assistance, and when it arrived conduct it in to the scene of the accident. But where to get assistance? He could go to Barrhill and contact Ayr,

139

a two-mile walk but a depot 36 miles away. His home station, Stranraer, was only 23 miles off, but to contact it would involve a $6\frac{1}{2}$-mile walk to Glenwhilly. It was truly a choice of evils, but he opted for Glenwhilly. He got his detonators and instructed the boy to put one on $\frac{1}{4}$-mile south, one at $\frac{1}{2}$-mile, and three, 10yd apart, at $\frac{3}{4}$-mile, reckoning distances by counting telegraph poles. The boy, who probably knew little of the distance to Glenwhilly, set off manfully, and seems to have placed his detonators correctly. Then he pressed on to the south.

Meanwhile Glenwhilly was getting a bit worried. A staff conference, (stationmaster and signalman) was held. A ganger, William McDowall, who lived at the station, listened-in over the fence, and suggested that he set off to search. He took his bicycle and rode up the road towards Barrhill, keeping the railway in view. At Miltonish farm he took the road to Markdow and got onto the railway at the occupation crossing. He was making his rather difficult way along the railway to the north, when about milepost $18\frac{1}{4}$ he met Allison, complete with tablet, heading wearily towards Glenwhilly.

Allison told of the derailment. Was the road damaged, the ganger wanted to know. The cleaner thought so, but he had been so concerned with the accident and his instructions about detonators that he had not paid much attention to that side of things. Yes, he remembered seeing broken chairs, so the ganger gave the boy his bicycle and his blessing, and pushed on himself on foot to the north. He passed the summit and started down the hill, and about milepost 15 he began to find serious damage. Between that point and the derailed engine he counted something like 600 broken sleepers with corresponding damage to chairs, and several rails buckled and displaced. He reached the engine and joined Dalrymple in the cab. After some conversation he went on for Barrhill.

About 3.00pm Stationmaster Clark of Barrhill got a message through to Assistant District Inspector Johnston at Girvan ($12\frac{1}{4}$ miles off) that all was not well on the moors. Johnston relayed the news to Ayr District Office, Kilmarnock Control, and other benevolent institutions. Then just after 4.00pm, he got definite word that there had been a derailment. He sought his colleague, Permanent Way Inspector Mitchell, and they got them a taxi and set off to Barrhill, arriving there 5.45pm. Meanwhile ganger William Kellie, of Barrhill, had thought that he would have a finger in the pie, and about 5.00pm he set out to walk up to the scene of the trouble. On the way, he met ganger McDowall from Glenwhilly and turned back with him. The two reached Barrhill about 5.50pm, just after the inspectors from Girvan.

All assembled in Barrhill booking office, and the inspectors decided to go up to the derailment. It was now a very dirty, dark night, so they had to wait to get lamps, but about 6.15pm the party of two inspectors and the two gangers set forth. They stumbled their way up in reasonably good time, but neither on the walk nor at the station previously did McDowall seem to have impressed upon Mitchell that the track was seriously damaged.

It was about 4.05pm when the forlorn figure of cleaner Allison cycled into Glenwhilly. Between cold, excitement and fatigue, he had to be revived with hot tea before he could give a coherent account of the situation. Stranraer was notified at once. Passed fireman Jock McLean was waiting with a Class 5 4–6–0 to hand over to the Corkerhill men to run the 4.20pm. He was given some carriages and dispatched on the 4.20pm time (approx) to run to Glenwhilly where it was hoped that a bus service could be started from Barrhill to exchange passengers with the stranded 12.30pm. Stranraer was notified to send up the tool van and a squad of lusty knaves. This was not easy with so many away at the match. Driver George ('Munch') Harvey was just booking-on at 4.45pm for the 7.55pm Milk, so he was grabbed for this trip. He was given Ayr Mogul No 2879, the tool van and two other vans of personnel, and left at 5.49pm. Stranraer's shedmaster, John Martin, accompanied the expedition. They got to Glenwhilly about 6.30pm. Jock McLean was there with his pseudo-4.20pm, waiting for the bus bringing the passengers from the 12.30pm over that awful road from Barrhill, after which he would have to take them to Stranraer, tender-first.

Allison, now restored, joined Harvey on No 2879, and gave very creditable directions. He said, 'We're lyin' just clear of the third snow fence from here, and go canny, Geordie, for there's a lot o' chairs broken.' They left Glenwhilly at 6.37pm. It would be about 6.45pm when the two inspectors plus the two gangers reached *Codrington*. It was now a vile night, extremely dark, with a very thick drizzle. One lamp was giving trouble. Mitchell had gone into the cab to fix that when those outside heard something. Unmistakably it was an engine approaching from the south! Ganger Kellie caught up his lamp and ran to the south end of the cutting from which he showed a red light. Bang-bang-bang – that was Harvey over the detonators at $\frac{3}{4}$-mile – a long pause, bang – that was the one at $\frac{1}{2}$-mile . . . then CRUNCH. That was No 2879 into the hole that *Codrington* had made.

Harvey said that he came over the summit and gently down until he struck the first three detonators. Then he came down to a crawl, expecting every second to be stopped by a red lamp, but no lamp could be seen. He had just exploded the detonator at $\frac{1}{2}$-mile when his engine and tender dropped off the track on all wheels. It was then 6.50pm. Six or seven minutes elapsed before anyone came up from *Codrington*.

With the second derailment the vans stopped with a bang. Out tumbled shedmaster Martin and the gang. They thought they had run into *Codrington*. Martin took a quick look at the situation. 'I can do nothing,' he said, 'till these three vans are lifted off her.' That meant rear-end assistance. That meant Stranraer. That meant Glenwhilly again for some poor fish! Harvey's regular fireman was away at the match; he had as deputy one James Marshall, known to all Stranraer as 'Buller' – a big, strong lad. It must have been past 7.00pm when he got his tablet and left, and at 8.31pm Marshall signed the book in Glenwhilly box, $6\frac{1}{2}$ miles away. He was soaked to the skin, and sorely impeded by his wet overalls clinging to his legs.

Stranraer was now in a proper spot. William Thorburn, leading fitter, nearly blew up when he heard of this latest misfortune. 'Ah've nae mair men or injins,' he protested to Control. 'A'

Above: Down train approaching Rockcliffe with LMS 2P 4-4-0 No 614 of Dumfries shed.
E. E. Smith

Below: Glasgow–Stranraer train just south of Lig viaduct, Pinwherry. LMS Horwich 2-6-0 No 2880.
F. R. Hebron

Above: Rail tour at Dunragit, 1961. Left to right: D. L. Smith, driver H. McGeorge (Corkerhill), retired drivers W. Cranston (Ayr) and A. McKnight (Stranraer).
E. M. Patterson

Below: Retired locomotive men at Stranraer, 1949. Standing left to right: leading fitter W. Thorburn, drivers J. Carruth, A. McKnight, E. Nish, W. Dunlop, H. McCloy. Seated: driver J. Thomson ('Sprig').
D. L. Smith collection

Stranraer an' his grannie's awa' at the match!' However, by some feat of conjuring he succeeded in producing both required ingredients, and at 9.38pm Jock McLean, just back from Glenwhilly with passengers off the connecting bus from the 12.30pm, with another Class 5X, No 5644, set out on yet another relief expedition. At 10.18pm he reached Glenwhilly, picked up Marshall, and went ahead with great circumspection. A surfaceman held them on about milepost $15\frac{1}{2}$, then walked ahead with a lamp till they came on the devastation from milepost 15. The vans were still on the track, so he coupled them on and at 11.15pm started back for Glenwhilly. As soon as it started away tender-first, a violent knock began beneath No 5644. McLean stopped and crawled underneath with a lamp, but could find nothing. He went on for a couple of miles; the knock became really alarming. Again he went underneath and again found nothing. He reached Glenwhilly without disintegration, rounded his vans, got them behind him, and back across the moor. Strangely, there was no knock when running forward. He reached the derailed Mogul at exactly midnight. Then shedmaster Martin got going. He used no jacks, just packing and ramps, and in 45 minutes from the start had No 2879 and tender back on the rails! It took some time to load the gear again, but they were away shortly after 2.00am, and booked off at Stranraer two hours later. At Stranraer they were told that an engine was off the road in the Cairnryan Exchange Sidings — they said that it could wait.

Things had not gone so briskly at the north end. The transfer of passengers between the 4.20pm at Glenwhilly and the 12.30pm at Barrhill was accomplished with difficulty, for the narrow, deep-rutted road was tearing the footboards of the bus, and after he got that run done, the busman said 'No more of *that!*' Will Scott left Barrhill with his train at 7.40pm, took it tender-first to Girvan, turned his engine there, but had to wait until nearly 9.00pm for a guard. They got to Glasgow eventually about 10.30pm.

Evidently it was thought that Martin's rough-and-ready re-railing was not good enough for an admiral, so for *Codrington* the Hurlford steam crane, 51 miles away, was ordered out at 8.20pm.

The breakdown train, with crane, left Hurlford at 9.55pm, but it was 12.45am before it got to Barrhill, and an hour later before it got up to *Codrington*. The tender of the derailed engine was uncoupled and brought back to Barrhill at 2.50am. *Codrington* was re-railed at 4.45am, and taken to Barrhill at 6.31am. Then came the task of re-making the track. A train of permanent way material left Motherwell at 11.33pm on Saturday, and a ballast train was dispatched from Irvine at 5.45am on Sunday, but it was a long job. The line was not opened till about 3.00pm on Monday, the 4.20pm being the first train through.

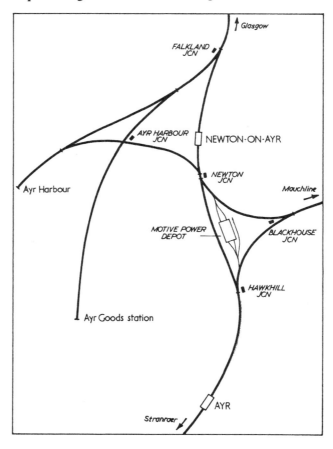

The arrangements for diverting the traffic during the hold-up were certainly comprehensive. Commencing with the 5.15pm ex-Glasgow on Saturday, all Glasgow–Stranraer trains were brought to Ayr station, then out again to the Mauchline line via Hawkhill and Blackhouse Junctions, thence to Stranraer via Dumfries. Trains in the opposite direction also took this route. From Ayr, rail connections were given to and from Girvan. South of that, a most elaborate bus service communicated with Stranraer, 1-via the Coast; 2-via Barrhill and Newton Stewart; 3-via Pinwherry, Colmonell and Ballantrae.

Sunday night provided some complications. Blackhouse (and possibly Hawkhill) were then switched out, so it was arranged to stop the 8.15pm Glasgow–Stranraer at Newton-on-Ayr, detach two Ayr coaches there, and run thence to the Mauchline line via Newton Junction and past Blackhouse. A special train was to be run out from Ayr at 9.06pm with Ayr–Stranraer passengers, and this train was to bring in the detached Ayr coaches. A bus was standing-by at Ayr station to make the Girvan connection. About 60 passengers and much luggage travelled from Ayr by this connection. Newton-on-Ayr station was not normally open on Sundays, and when Inspector Rogerson went out with this train he discovered that no one had arranged for Newton station to be open and lit. Inspector and guards had to tackle the job of transferring passengers (and luggage) to the opposite platform, not to speak of detaching and collecting the Ayr coaches, all in darkness. They got back to Ayr with sighs of relief, to find that the bus driver had become confused by what the ticket collector had told him, and that he was away now to Newton!

With Stranraer motive power depot cut off from direct rail or bus connection with the affected area, and Ayr 36 miles away to the north, the provision and relief of enginemen was not a simple task. The crew of the 1.00pm Girvan–Stranraer, which had started all this, had booked on at Stranraer at 8.00am. They were relieved at Pinmore about 12 hours later and promised a lift home by a special Girvan–Stranraer bus going via Barrhill and Newton Stewart. They waited two hours in pouring rain at the road end to discover that someone had sent this bus via the coast road, and they had to hire a taxi to Stranraer.

On the Sunday, two officials of the engineer's department went up by car to a point on the Barrhill–Glenwhilly road almost opposite to the scene of the derailments, and walked the mile or so across to the railway. Before they could return, a mist had come down. They got to the road, but at a point to the north of the car, and walked almost into Barrhill in the belief that the car had been stolen.

No mechanical defect could be found to account for *Codrington*'s derailment, so came the old, well-tried verdict, 'the driver was going too hard.' There was, helpfully, a 45mph restriction round curves at that point. Dalrymple denied that he was exceeding that limit, and I do not think that it is at all likely that he was doing so.

At Stranraer there was naturally much discussion concerning the cause. Those who had travelled by the heavy football special recalled that their progress up to the summit had been somewhat laboured, and that thereafter they had gone down the banks in very lively fashion. It was thought that the heavy engine (another Class 5X) had strained the track on some of the curves. Dalrymple's big stiff tender, pushing ahead of his engine, would not have helped matters. His coupled wheels may have struck a weak spot. Suffice it to add, in conclusion, that Stranraer *lost* the match, 5–2. The weary supporters got home (via Dumfries) at 2.30am on Sunday.

11

The Hold-up at the Cairn

The second series of events took place in December 1947, on the main Carlisle–Glasgow line of the old G&SW, between the stations of Sanquhar and New Cumnock. Distances from Sanquhar are shown as under:

	Miles	Chains
Sanquhar station	0	00
Gateside signalbox	1	02
Kirkconnel station	3	27
Intermediate block signals (Upper Cairn)	7	17
New Cumnock station	10	63

For all this distance the line is in the upper valley of the River Nith; between Kirkconnel and New Cumnock this valley runs east to west. The railway is on the north side of the valley, rather lonely country, with few dwellings near the line, and the main road (A76) on the other side of the valley about a mile away. From Sanquhar to Kirkconnel the grades are easy, then comes a four-mile climb at about 1 in 200. The last $3\frac{1}{2}$ miles to New Cumnock are virtually level. In 1947 there were track water troughs about $1\frac{1}{2}$ miles east of New Cumnock.

In 1947, all of this main line was double track. The section between Kirkconnel and New Cumnock was a long one, and it was formerly divided by a signalbox at Upper Cairn, 3.9 miles from Kirkconnel. This box was burned down in 1939, and in 1941 was replaced by intermediate block signals on approximately the same site. These were of the 'approach lit' variety; the down line signals were controlled from Kirkconnel box, and the up signals from New Cumnock. Local railwaymen referred to these signals

149

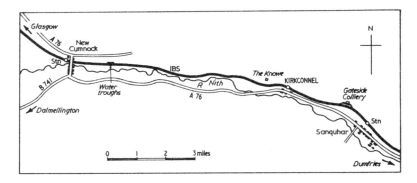

as 'The Lights'. Officially they were called 'IBS', and I shall use this term here.

There are extensive coal measures in this district, and in 1947 there were active collieries at Gateside, a mile from Sanquhar, and at Kirkconnel, adjacent to the station. Their coal went mainly to Ayr harbour for shipment, and was handled by trains under the jurisdiction of Kilmarnock Control Area. Each of those trains bore a code number with the prefix K.

There were water columns at the station platforms at New Cumnock and Sanquhar, and engines fitted for picking up water could use the troughs, but no water was available at Kirkconnel station.

The date was 17 December 1947. The train mainly concerned was K151, which was booked to leave Ayr Harbour at 12.55pm and run to Sanquhar, returning from there at 4.05pm. On the date in question it was running about $2\frac{1}{4}$ hours behind those times, but this had no bearing on the events which followed.

Driver Hugh Hood, of Ayr, was on K151 on this date, with engine No 17615, a Caley class 3F 0–6–0. When he got to Kirkconnel, he found there driver Hugh Gordon, of Ayr, on train K153 with Mogul No 2927, and there was an order from Control that Hood was to exchange engines with Gordon. They did so. Gordon told Hood that No 2927 was in good order, with fire newly cleaned, but that since the tank was filled at New Cumnock on the outward journey, he had done two hours' heavy shunting, and that Hood had better check up on the water, as the tender gauge was not working.

150

Driver Hood got No 2927 and his train of empties, and set off tender-first for Sanquhar. Calling at Gateside colliery he detached his empties and got 16 loads which he took to Sanquhar. Those were for destinations to the south. Gateside box switched-out fairly early, Sanquhar was open round the clock, any train going south could collect those as convenient.

At Sanquhar Hood's fireman, John Brechany, examined the tank and found the water level about $2\frac{1}{2}$ft from the top. This was sufficient to take them back to New Cumnock. Hood examined his sanders and found that none of them was working. With a piece of wire he managed to clear the driving ones, but he could not get the leading ones to work. Then they went off with the van only to Gateside colliery, there attaching 46 of coal (equal to 47 mineral) and one of goods. This latter one was the only excess over maximum engine load.

All went well until they passed Kirkconnel at 6.21pm. Then they got on to the up-grade, and bad slipping began. It had rained, then frozen, then rained again, and the rail was about as bad as could be. They kept going, slipping very badly and taking an awful time, and presently they stuck altogether. No one could tell when this was. The driver said it was so dark and they had been so long on the road. The guard's watch had stopped and he had no key to wind it. When they stopped, the guard, James Thomson of Ayr Harbour, went forward and found Hood and the fireman taking sand out of the boxes. They sanded ahead for about 100yd and Hood said that they would have another try at getting away. They got on all right till they cleared the sanded patch, then the locomotive slipped again. They staggered on and finally stuck dead at a point stated to be about a mile short of the IBS distant. It was then 8.00pm. The guard armed with a Wrong Line Order form, went forward. Hood took the Wrong Line Order, and told the guard to cut off 22 wagons, and said that he would try to get to New Cumnock with them. The guard told him to stop at the IBS when he got there and report the situation to Kirkconnel. Away went Hood, the locomotive slipping badly. The guard proceeded to protect the remainder of his train at both ends.

151

James Beck, the signalman at Kirkconnel, had been worrying for quite a while. Passing Kirkconnel at 6.21pm, Hood's train should have reached New Cumnock by 6.41pm. At 6.47pm, the 12.13pm freight from Carlisle to Millikenpark arrived at Kirkconnel, and still there was no word of K151 being even as far as the IBS. It was a still night, and going to the door signalman Beck could hear No 2927 coughing away, slipping, but still going. He telephoned signalman John Beattie at New Cumnock to that effect. The 5.00pm passenger from Carlisle was now approaching, so they put the 12.13pm freight through the crossover and into the up loop.

Stationmaster Hugh Mair of Kirkconnel was off duty, but sitting in his house at 7.16pm he heard the 5.00pm ex-Carlisle whistling for the road and not getting it. The signalbox is a little way from the station, so he crossed to the shunters' bothy and from there telephoned signalman Beck, who told him that K151 had passed him at 6.21pm and was not yet at 'The Lights'. The 5.38pm ex-Glasgow was just coming in, so the stationmaster ran to the platform and asked the crew of that train if they had seen anything of K151, but they said not. Mair went to the box and telephoned such news as he had to Kilmarnock Control. He then went to the GPO telephone and called-up the farmer at The Knowe, about two miles out and near the line. The farmer's wife answered and said that she could hear a train in the direction of Nethertown. It was 'taking two or three puffs and then dying away.' That seemed a fairly apt description of the hapless K151, so the stationmaster got back to the signalbox, called Control again, and recommended that the next train through the section from the New Cumnock end should be asked to stop in the section and investigate.

The stationmaster's first message at 7.35pm was the first news that Control had received that anything was wrong. The Controller on duty seems to have decided at once that if assistance was required it must be provided in the rear, from the Kirkconnel end. But first, communication must be established with K151. The engine of K179 had been shunting at New

Cumnock since 6.45pm, but apparently was deemed incapable of intellectual work such as this. The 6.40pm freight Woodhill (Kilmarnock) to Carlisle was by then passing Auchinleck. The signalman at New Cumnock was instructed to stop the 6.40pm, tell the driver to investigate the matter of the K151, and if necessary convey the guard of K151 to Kirkconnel. The 6.40pm, with Class 5X No 5716, was stopped at New Cumnock at 7.50pm, got the instructions and proceeded at 7.58pm.

At 8.29pm came the first voice from the void. Driver Hood called-up from the IB home signal telephone to say that he had got that far with his first portion, and that the second portion was lying 500yd south of Bridge No 200, a marvellous bit of pin-pointing on a dark night. I do not know if that information was of much use to Control, which probably did not know that the old G&SW possessed 200 bridges. Mair told Hood to stand by until he had reported to Control, so at 8.33pm Control was informed that the engine of K151 was on its way to New Cumnock with its first 22 wagons, and was at present standing at the IBS.

Control said that this would not do at all. Assistance *must* be provided from the rear, and as Hood was in possession of a guard's Wrong Line Order, he must propel back to the remainder of his train, and that an assistant engine would be sent up from Kirkconnel to push the whole outfit through to New Cumnock. Mair informed Hood of this. I do not quite know what the trouble was here. Possibly some complication concerning the IBS and the track-circuiting, so that a man coming back wrong road for the second portion would upset the electrical gear.

At 8.35pm the 6.40pm ex-Woodhill stopped opposite Kirkconnel box and the driver stated that 'the guard of K151 had informed him that they had divided their train,' but the guard had not come with him. To what phantom they had been speaking I do not know, for the guard of K151 said that he saw the 6.40pm stop in the section, but at the time he was well forward protecting his train, and they never contacted him.

When Hughie Hood was told that after all his labour in getting his first portion hauled up to the IBS he had to go right back to where he started he would be blazing, I am sure. But he had a worse packet coming, for when he got back from the telephone to the engine, fireman Brechany says 'The injector's blown back — the tank's dry!' Hughie gave one despairing look and fled for the telephone again.

Just after 8.00pm, chief controller Lamont, off duty, dropped in to the Kilmarnock Control office, and found his staff gravely concerned about the fate of a coal train which had vanished without trace in the remote valley between Kirkconnel and New Cumnock. Lamont had no time to waste on speculation. He ordered single-line working to be started on the up road. In truth it was time something was done, for the hold-up was by now pretty fierce. The 5.00pm passenger ex-Carlisle had been at Kirkconnel since 7.15pm, Sanquhar had been holding the 2.10pm freight from Carlisle to Elderslie since 6.56pm, and the 5.20pm express ex-Carlisle since 7.53pm. The 2.54pm freight from Carlisle to College had been at Mennock IBS from 8.00pm, the 6.50pm express from Carlisle at Carronbridge from 8.15pm, and the 3.50pm freight had been lying at Thornhill since 7.36pm. In addition fitted freight No 1, the famous 6.25pm College to Carlisle, had been held at New Cumnock since 8.15pm. Everyone had started chasing around on the single-line question when signalman Beck from Kirkconnel blew them all endways with the news that No 2927 was now a complete failure.

Stationmaster Mair at Kirkconnel was told to grab the engine of the 12.13pm freight and get going forthwith into the section to the rescue. Signalman Beck was told to telephone driver Hood at the IBS and tell him to get back and warn the guard that assistance would be coming from the rear. Signalman Beck did just this, but something mysterious seems to have happened to the message, for the one that reached the palpitating Hughie at the IBS was 'Go back and tell the guard that *single-line working is being started on the up line.*' So back Hughie went to the engine, repeated to the fireman this story about single-line working, told him to get cracking and dump the fire, and then beat it for the rear.

Stationmaster Mair got the engine off the 12.13pm. It was

Class 5X No 5560, powerful, but a long-legged express engine, and Mair felt a little dubious of its ability to push 800 tons or so of train plus a dead engine. So before he left he got from signalman Beck a Wrong Line Order in case he had to draw them back to Kirkconnel. They entered the section at 8.45pm.

Guard Thomson, of K151, was out at the rear of his train when he heard what he took to be his own engine returning from New Cumnock. To his surprise an engine came up from the rear, and stationmaster Mair, dismounting, was able to tell Thomson of the catastrophe that had overtaken his own engine. No 5560 was duly coupled up to the rear, but now the difficulty was to find the first portion in the dark, so the guard and stationmaster started to walk towards New Cumnock; 200yd ahead, however, they met driver Hood walking back. Hood was asked to hand over his guard's Wrong Line Order, then it was arranged that the guard go back and tell No 5560's driver to begin pushing very gently, while the stationmaster and driver Hood walked just ahead of them and guided them forward. So presently the stationmaster and the driver tramped away into the rain and the murk. Hood apparently spoke of the single-line working, and Mair said that he had heard nothing about it. So they tramped on, and presently discovered to their consternation that they had lost the second portion! Hood pushed on to find if his engine was still in one piece, while Mair retraced his steps, and had got back almost to his starting point when he met the cavalcade, only just leaving. This time he took no chances, but walked alongside all the way up.

With all this going on it was 9.43pm when they got buffered-up to the first portion. Mair asked Hood to report from the IBS telephone to Kirkconnel that they were coupled-up and off for New Cumnock, then when he had done so to show 'a moving white light.' Mair returned to No 5560; at 9.47pm the agreed light appeared and they started. It was not as bad as anticipated – the first portion anyway must have reached the level. They got inside clear at New Cumnock at 10.35pm.

The question of opening single-line working on the up line was raised by controller Lamont shortly after his arrival in Control office at 8.00pm, but the first intimation of it to the world outside seems to have been about 8.30pm, when Lamont got on the telephone to the signalman at New Cumnock and told him to contact the stationmaster there, Andrew Hannah, who was having his half-day off. He was though in his home when about 8.40pm a shunter called and summoned him to the signalbox. Hannah got to the box about 8.50pm, and was instructed by Lamont as to the general situation and told to proceed to Kirkconnel and open single-line working. Hannah made out his forms, then boarded the engine of the 6.25pm fitted freight, with which train he travelled to Kirkconnel. They did not stop in the section, but turned their lamps on the battleground as they passed. This puzzled Mair, who remarked that 'surely that's something like a pilotman on single-line working.' On arrival at Kirkconnel at 9.23pm, Hannah proceeded to the signalbox and said that he had come to open single-line working. 'Oh,' said signalman Beck, 'you can't do that there 'ere,' pointing out that Mair was in possession of a Wrong Line Order for the down line. Any down train transferring to the up line at Kirkconnel would have to draw far forward on the down line before backing through the crossover, and Mair, with his Wrong Line Order, could come back on top of them. Hannah no doubt said 'That's torn it,' and at 9.26pm he telephoned signalman Beattie at New Cumnock to cancel the form in his possession and withdraw the protection. That, emphatically, was that. Hannah returned to New Cumnock by the 5.00pm ex-Carlisle.

K151 would clear the IBS about 9.51pm, and at 10.00pm signalman Beck allowed the 5.00pm ex-Carlisle forward to the IBS. When K151 reached New Cumnock at 10.35pm, the 5.00pm went forward, the 5.20pm express followed it to the IBS, and the process of breaking-up the traffic jam went on steadily as detailed in the summary of delays to trains which follows this narrative. Mair returned to Kirkconnel at 11.25pm, went to the signalbox, handed-in his Wrong Line Order and had it cancelled. Then he went home and put his feet up. It had been quite a night!

Delays to trains

Passenger trains

5.0pm   Carlisle to St Enoch
Kirkconnel 7.15pm until 10.00pm

5.20pm   Carlisle to St Enoch
Sanquhar 7.33pm until 10.00pm. Kirkconnel 10.09pm
until 10.37pm

6.50pm   Carlisle to St Enoch
Carronbridge 8.15pm until 10.09pm. Mennock IBS
10.27pm until 10.44pm

Freight trains

12.13pm   Carlisle to Millikenpark. Engine No 5560. Arrived
Kirkconnel 6.47pm. Train detached in up loop, engine
forward to propel K151 to New Cumnock, 8.45pm

2.10pm   Carlisle to Elderslie. Engine No 5119. Sanquhar
6.56pm until 11.24pm. Light engine to Kirkconnel to
work forward 12.13pm. Attaching train Kirkconnel
11.27pm to 11.50pm. 12.13pm was terminated
Hurlford Moss.

2.54pm   Carlisle to College. Engine No 3996. Mennock IBS
8.00pm until 10.15, Sanquhar 10.40pm until 10.53pm
− 2.10pm ahead.

3.50pm   Carlisle to Polmadie. Engine No 5455. Thornhill
7.36pm until 10.50pm. Terminated at Hurlford Moss.

3.10pm   Carlisle to Kilbirnie. Engine No 5100. Closeburn
8.46pm until 10.45pm. Carronbridge 11.27pm until
11.44pm − 3.50pm ahead. Mennock IBS 11.53pm
until 11.57pm−3.50pm ahead. Terminated at
Kilmarnock Long Lyes.

5.20pm   Carlisle to Ayr. Engine No 2809. Auldgirth 8.58pm until 10.48pm, Closeburn 11.02pm until 11.15pm − 3.10pm ahead, Carronbridge 11.50pm until 12.01. Terminated at Mauchline.

8.55pm   Carlisle to Elderslie. Engine No 5309. Holywood 9.41pm until 10.46pm − 5.20pm ahead; Auldgirth 11.02pm until 11.14pm. Closeburn 11.28pm until 11.38pm, Thornhill 11.48pm until 12.04pm Carronbridge 12.18pm until 12.33pm, Sanquhar 12.54pm until 1.08pm.

6.40pm   Woodhill to Carlisle. Engine No 5716. New Cumnock 7.50pm until 7.58pm − instructions to driver and guard, Kirkconnel 8.35pm until 8.37pm − delivering message.

6.25pm   College to Carlisle. Engine No 5084, New Cumnock 8.15pm until 9.00pm − uncertainty concerning K151, Kirkconnel − setting down pilotman, 9.23pm until 9.26pm.

8.50pm   Woodhill to Carlisle. Engine No 2739. Auchinleck 9.31pm until 10.22pm. Held for passing of 9.05pm express St Enoch to Carlisle.

C92   (Carlisle Control Area train). Engine No 17657. Train cancelled and engine and van home to Dumfries.

K179   New Cumnock 6.27pm until 11.44pm, then hauled dead engine of K151 to Mauchline.

12

LMS Finale

Class 5X 4–6–0s were the predominant power on the Stranraer road for the first two years of war, then about 1942 the Class 5 4–6–0s began to filter in. They were all visitors, mostly from Kingmoor, some grand engines among them. Nos 5151–3/5 were particularly good. On 14 November 1942 Mulholland and Dodds had No 5153 on the 4.20pm. With 206 tons their running time to Girvan was only 62 minutes 33 seconds. They were then loaded up to 346 tons, and made Maybole in eight seconds over their booked 18 minutes. Jimmy McCreadie with No 5152 and 206 tons topped Dalrymple Junction without falling below 35mph, albeit with full open regulator and 50 per cent cut-off! I saw Jimmy coming flying down past Cassillis with No 5155 in centre gear and the knock no worse than usual. No 5100 was another good engine. On the 12.30pm, with a light load of 146 tons from Girvan, John Craven, son of Adam, went to Stranraer in a running time of 60 minutes 38 seconds, booked time 73 minutes.

Corkerhill got its first Class 5s in 1943, a mixed bunch, of course. Nos 5047/9 were rather poor, No 5047 definitely a weakling. No 5194 never shone very brilliantly on any run of mine. Then Nos 5489–91 arrived new. I never heard any great praise of that trio, but in 1945 the 4900 series began to come out. The Corkerhill boys had three freight turns to Carlisle at that time and were thrilled. Davie Wightman had No 4900 on the 6.25pm ex-College – 38 wagons and van, 16 fitted. He said that the engine was marvellous; time and again he had to restrain it to keep within the quite tight schedule. He left Dumfries and was through Annan in 20 minutes.

The Class 5s had peculiar traits, however. Sam McKnight had

one on the 5.10pm one night in 1939 with eight on. Jock Thomson had built up too big a fire at St Enoch, and did not fire again until passing Troon Goods, 34.9 miles. Then in 1947 they tested No 4995 with the coal-weighing tender, on the Stranraer road, and it was doing the job on 34lb of coal per mile. Those were excellent performances, but they seemed to be exceptional. In general, both Class 5 and Class 5X locomotives had good healthy appetites for coal. I remarked on this to a fireman who was shovelling hard: 'She likes her meat,' he said. On 18 April 1942 I went to Stranraer. Most unusually for that period there was a compound on the 8.55am. It was that hardy annual from Corkerhill, No 1110. At Girvan I was bidden to the footplate. 'She's rough and she's dirty,' I was warned. The engine was all that, but what impressed me was that the fireman had so little to do. I am not exaggerating when I say that the run-down compound was burning no more than two-thirds of the coal that a Class 5 or 5X would have burned with a similar load.

The Class 5s were good, and could be brilliant, but oh, that *knock*! I am told that they never lost it, right to the very last of them. It could be very terrible at times. The worst I ever encountered was on No 5487 of Polmadie. It was not a knock, it was a positive explosion every time the wheel came round. I thought it a bit ironical that Sir William Stanier should have to leave his post and go out to India to advise on the trouble with certain Indian engines when he could not cure the trouble on his own at home.

Heavy traffic continued for some time after the war. There was little or no increase in the train services provided, and crowds of service people were still travelling. Milk traffic from Northern Ireland to Glasgow continued very busily. This was a traffic begun in wartime. It grew to such dimensions as to require a special ship, and this had to be diverted to Cairnryan port to ease the burden at Stranraer. War Department engines brought the milk train up to Cairnryan Junction, and it left for Glasgow about 7.40pm. The return empties left Glasgow South Side about 6.30pm. There were some heavy loads. Jimmy McKay of

Corkerhill with No 5575 is said to have worked a train of 372 tons to Girvan unaided, and I saw Gus McBride on the milk empties with Mogul No 2914 and 24 vans.

It was not a very bright time, this post-war year, with run-down stock, poor coal, and still heavy traffic, but it had its diverting incidents. Did you ever hear of the night they lost the Paddy?

Christmas Eve, 1945. The Paddy left Stranraer for Glasgow at its booked time of 10.15pm. It was due to stop in Girvan 11.20pm to 11.25pm, and at Ayr 11.55pm to11.57pm. The engine was Class 5X No 5643, driver Alex Connor of Corkerhill. The load is not remembered, but was likely to have been five corridor coaches.

On duty that night at Ayr station was inspector John Rogerson. About 11.30pm he telephoned Girvan and was told that the Paddy had left there on time. Between Ayr No 2 and Girvan No 1 boxes, 21 miles, there were then 13 block posts, but at that time of night only two were open, Belmont, one mile from Ayr, and Kilkerran, 13.4 miles. Both of these boxes controlled level-crossings, and were treble-shifted.

About 11.50pm Rogerson left his office and went out on to the platform. 11.55pm came, but no sign of the Paddy. Christmas morning came in, he waited till about 12.10am, then went back to the office and telephoned Belmont. Belmont reported that the Paddy had passed Kilkerran all right, but had not reached there. It was a dark night but very still, and he had been listening at the open window but could hear no sound of a train.

At 12.20am Rogerson telephoned Ayr locomotive depot and reported the matter. About 1.10am a Mogul came up tender-first with Russell, night foreman, and a fitter. Rogerson joined them and they proceeded to Belmont box. There they procured a Wrong Line Order, lest they should find the up line blocked and have to return. Then they pushed on, very cautiously, into the unknown, all staring ahead into the darkness. They got to the top of the hill at Dalrymple Junction, $3\frac{1}{4}$ miles, and had found nothing. Now downhill, still very gently, and they were just through Dalrymple station when someone sang out that he had seen a light. So it was, a wavering white light, coming towards them. It was carried by the fireman of the Paddy, which had broken-down about $\frac{2}{3}$-mile south of Dalrymple station.

It appeared that after passing Kilkerran, trouble with the vacuum brake developed, and the train was finally dragged to a standstill within sight of Dalrymple down distant. A hurried examination revealed in one of the brake pipes a hole which had been plugged with wood; the plug had fallen out, hence the trouble. Another plug was manufactured, vacuum was raised, and at the restart the centre big-end on the engine flew to pieces!

The foreman and the fitter descended to find out whether the engine could be made movable in a reasonable time. If not, the coaches would have to be drawn off from the rear, so the Mogul carried on south. At Maybole they stopped and Rogerson got the stationmaster out to open the signal box and thus shorten the section should they have to pull the train back. Then they went on to Kilkerran.

At Kilkerran, Rogerson telephoned Belmont and told the signalman there to cancel his wrong line order. Then from the Kilkerran signalman he got a wrong line order to provide for a pull-back. They then proceeded on the down line for the 8.6 miles to the stranded train. There they got a good report, and after a short time the engine was declared ready to be moved. They were all ready to go when someone remembered that there was a catch-point about there. However, no long search was necessary; No 5643 had most considerately sat down right on top of it!

The Mogul buffered-up in the rear and pushed the train and the dead engine gently up to Dalrymple Junction and then down to Belmont. There they stopped and Rogerson cancelled his wrong line order by telephone to Kilkerran. Stopping again at Ayr No 2, rounding the train, they put the engine into the Long Lye and drew forward into Ayr station at 3.40am. The Mogul took the train on to Glasgow; a Caley 0—6—0 came up and took the cripple to Ayr shed.

After that I hope that inspector Rogerson had a happy Christmas. It was a good night's work, deserving great praise.

Instead, he got a severe reprimand for having cancelled his wrong line orders by telephone – he should have delivered them *in person*. Today Wrong Line Orders do not exist and assisting moves like this (sometimes with signal boxes 50 or so miles away) are organised by ... *telephone!*

Throughout the second world war, there had been stored in various remote areas of Britain, poison-gas shells, in case the enemy should take up that form of warfare. After the war, those shells were disposed of. They were loaded on to obsolete merchant ships which were then escorted out to mid-ocean and scuttled. Cairnryan port handled a number of such cargoes. The shells were taken to Cairnryan in somewhat casual fashion, by ordinary freight trains, and one night a grave disaster was narrowly averted.

The 11.35pm freight College to Stranraer had a Class 5X with driver Peter ('Bud') Fisher of Corkerhill. The load from Ayr consisted of two vans, 18 wagons of gas shells, and brake van. The 11.35pm was followed by the 1.10am ex-Falkland Junction which, at a crossing point, usually Barrhill, met and exchanged crews with a freight from Stranraer. Willie Cranston of Ayr was on the 1.10am, with a Caley Class 3F 0–6–0, and with nine wagons of gas shells in the make-up.

The 1.10am got to Girvan and was held up at Girvan No 1, as the 11.35pm was taking water at the passenger station Presently the 11.35pm departed and the 1.10am drew up to the station and began to take water in its turn. The engine was right opposite Girvan No 2 box; the signalman on duty was Tom Walker, brother of Johnnie.

It was a bad night, storming and raining and very dark. The fireman could not keep a light burning on the tender-top, and was hard put to stand upright. Rails were bad that night; up in Glendoune they could hear Bud Fisher's engine coughing, spluttering and slipping and sometimes coming to a stand. Then suddenly down the hill out of the darkness came a train. It roared through the station, shot past and was gone ...

Yes, the 11.35pm had broken away, behind the tender. Down

came 18 wagons of poison gas – and another nine sitting in the station. But Girvan was saved. As soon as the 11.35pm was clear on to the single line, Tom Walker had carefully set his points for the down road, so the runaway went past without harm. It was a narrow escape. They tell me the guard of the 11.35pm never got quite over it; he left railway service soon after.

We had suffered privations during the war period, but in my opinion they were surpassed by those of that arctic winter of early 1947. I know that Ayrshire, for the first two months, had had no snowfall comparable with that in England, but there was the cold. For 50 days the wind blew steadily from the east. Food was rigorously rationed, and fuel was short. In our six-room house we huddled in the kitchen, its doors and window padded against draughts, and tended our one fire. We gathered coal from the streets, spillings from the gasworks carts. Snow fell, but only enough to encumber the streets with foul slush. Then on Wednesday 12 March, we had the father and mother of a snowstorm.

In some places it began suddenly. At Glenwhilly at 5.00pm there were but wandering flakes of snow; by 7.00pm the station was cowering beneath a blizzard which was to make history. Through a shrieking gale and with drifts mounting up the 5.10pm from Glasgow made its way south. It had Class 5X No 5728 and a train crew of Stranraer men, George Hannay, driver, Henry Lightbody, fireman and John Wright, guard. They had four corridors, with 57 passengers. As they stopped at Barrhill, Hannay thought of topping-up his tank, in case of subsequent delays, but just then he got the rightaway, and did not do so. He regretted it later.

At 7.35pm they got to Glenwhilly, and there had to wait. Bud Fisher on the College goods had long since left New Luce, and was still battling away in the section. They waited an hour at Glenwhilly, seventy minutes, eighty, then came word from New Luce that the goods had returned there, having failed to get through the drifts.

A snowplough was now necessary before the 5.10pm could

attempt a passage. Snowploughs were scarce, for Scotland had been lending generously to England. It was 11.00pm before one got south to Glenwhilly and drove on into the New Luce section. At two minutes to midnight New Luce gave out-of-section for the plough. At 12.03am the 5.10pm resumed its journey.

Anxiously the Glenwhilly signalman watched his clock. Eight minutes should have taken the 5.10pm down the $4\frac{1}{2}$ miles to New Luce, but eight minutes went by, fifteen, half-an-hour – still no word of it. It was just on 1.00am when a burly, snow-shrouded figure plunged in out of the storm, guard John Wright. The 5.10pm was stuck fast in the rock cutting half-a-mile south of Glenwhilly.

This was bad news, but Wright reported the train well heated and lighted, and in his van a consignment of foodstuffs for the NAAFI canteens. Authority was given to issue those to passengers and crew, and big Jock tramped resolutely back to his train. Food was doled out and the passengers settled down in reasonable comfort in their snowy prison. All night the driver and fireman remained on the engine and kept the heating going.

Dawn broke on a Thursday of screaming gale and snow, which never ceased to whirl and drift. Stationmaster James Blackwood of Glenwhilly collected his limited forces and at 7.00am a supply of hot tea was carried perilously up to the half-buried train. No doubt the tea lost some of its heat on the journey, but it was the best that could be done. Three times during the day those devoted carriers made this exhausting journey. With one such party fireman Lightbody returned to Glenwhilly with his tablet, but he collapsed on the way and had to be carried to the signalbox. By noon came a cruel moment when the engine tender tank became empty. The fire had to be thrown out; the steam heating was finished. Towards night a new peril developed, for the train windows began to crack from the pressure of the snow. One window caved-in, and two passengers were cut rather badly. Thursday night closed in grimly. The train was deathly cold; the lights had gone out. Away to the north, another snowplough was ten miles off, stuck fast between Pinwherry and Barrhill; to the south, the Stranraer plough had reached New Luce, but had gone back to Stranraer for water, and the cuts would be filling up again.

With Friday 14 March came an easing. The storm died down; even a spark of sun came out. No time was lost. Fires were built up in the Glenwhilly houses, in the booking office, the waiting room and in a surfacemen's hut. Then the passengers were escorted down to the station. There, in shelter and warmth, the Glenwhilly folk tended and fed them. This was not easy, for Thursday was their ration day, the vans had been unable to get through, and their own larders were getting low. Fuel, too, was running out, and a sledge expedition had to be organised to bring coal from No 5728's tender.

About 5.00pm on Friday afternoon came the first contact with the outer world. A Stranraer guard, Harry Rice, walked in from the south, and reported that a train of workers had reached a point some three miles from Glenwhilly. He said it was possible for fit persons to make their way to the train. Thirty-two passengers and the three trainmen agreed to return with him, and Guard Rice led his pilgrim band down through the wilderness. A sore floundering it must have been, for the railway was lost among the drifts, and they had to cut across country, but they got to the train before dark and to Stranraer that night.

On the Saturday, all hands mustered in a final rescue party. A squad of police, led by the chief constable, and a large body of German prisoners-of-war made their way up to Glenwhilly. The remaining passengers were brought down to a relief train, German prisoners with stretchers carrying the older passengers over the worst drifts. All had reached Stranraer by afternoon. One lady was so grateful to her four German bearers that she later entertained them to dinner at a Stranraer hotel.

If the people marooned in the train had had a tough time, their rescuers did not have it easy either. On Thursday 13 March Stranraer got out two snowploughs. One was attached to Caley Class 3F 0–6–0 No 17626, with driver George Robertson and fireman Willie Darroch, the latter just back from wartime driving on the Trans-Iranian Railway. Coupled to them was Mogul No

2739, driver Davie Galloway and fireman Jock Harding. They were delayed for ages at Dunragit while Authority made up its mind which line to tackle, then they were sent the Girvan line. It was a rough job, for No 17626 had a slack tender coupling, and every time they struck a drift the tender rammed the engine and sent them reeling, then the Mogul would ram the tender. They got only a little way beyond New Luce, then had to return to Stranraer for water. Providentially, No 17626 had run hot, so the plough was transferred to that old Millisle stalwart, No 17440, with the tender cab.

They began again the next day, Friday, Galloway with Class 5X No 5644 in place of the Mogul. The drifts above New Luce were terrible. Engines and men were nearly smothered, and the cab windows were burst in on No 5644. Willie Kilpatrick came up with a train of German prisoners, who helped by digging. By Friday evening they were well up to the start of the Swan's Neck. All day Saturday they were ploughing and digging their way round the Neck, and on Sunday they reached the snowed-up train.

Meanwhile the Ayr boys had not been idle. They likewise had a Caley Class 3F 0–6–0 on the plough with a Mogul to push. Up about the Chirmorie they charged a drift with great vigour, but it was frozen hard. The plough broke, got under the wheels of the 0–6–0 and put it off the track. The 2–6–0s crew, blinded by torrents of snow, kept thundering away and pushing the derailed 0–6–0 till they could push no longer. So that was a nice job for the breakdown men, and a sore hindrance to progress from the north. Then there was the task of excavating No 5728 and its train; engine, tender and coaches had to be dragged out one by one. It was Thursday, 20 March before the line was open through to Girvan.

The second snowplough at Stranraer was given the task of clearing the Port Road, and it got out on Thursday 13 March, ahead of the Edinburgh milk. Dick Conchie was on the plough. They made fair progress until things got bad after Gatehouse and they stuck dead in a drift somewhere about the Big Fleet. They dropped the fire and went back to Gatehouse station. Big Andy McColm and Geordie Skimming were on the milk train, and they stuck in a cut somewhere below Creetown. They probably sought refuge in the van, and when the weather lulled on Friday set off to walk to Newton Stewart. They were overtaken by Dick Conchie and his mate. The four enginemen were lodged in a Newton Stewart hotel, but the guard of the milk train refused to stay in Newton Stewart, and tramped on to Stranraer, 23 miles. They breed them tough in Galloway.

Stranraer was inaccessible both by rail and road during this period. One of the cross-channel ships, however, made several special trips from Stranraer to Gourock, and the men of the College goods on 12 March got home eventually by this means.

That was in March 1947. It was succeeded by a summer of periods of almost tropical heat. In July of that summer the King and Queen paid a state visit to Scotland. The LMS was much involved with the Royal itinerary, and great care and thought went to the planning. Never was there such careful scrutiny of arrangements beforehand, and never did things go so wrong!

It was truly maddening. Every day produced its catalogue of little things, mistakes, usually made by folks who had never been known to make a mistake in their lives, utterly unforeseen delays, misunderstandings. But the crowning disaster came on 21 July, when the Royal Train was scheduled to leave Ibrox about 4.30pm and proceed via Paisley and Elderslie to the Greenock line, for the night was to be spent at Upper Port Glasgow, a little goods station on the moors above the towns of the lower Clyde.

A Corkerhill driver was on the 9.18am from Greenock Princes Pier. As he swept up the hill from Cart Junction his eye wandered to the left and he saw, across country, Elderslie No 1 home signal off. Unfortunately he did not look above his head, where Elderslie No 2 home signal for the Greenock road was very much ON. Elderslie No 1 was off for the 9.00am from Ayr. So, as the 9.18am came up to the junction, the 9.00am went headlong into the side of the Greenock coaches. Class 2P 4-4-0 No 648 of Ayr went over on its side. Jock Sargent, driving, was not hurt, but Tom McLean the fireman was underneath the engine with a broken collar-bone. There were about half-a-dozen injured, none very seriously, but three out of the four tracks were blocked; only the up slow remained clear. This on a Fair Monday, the day on which Glasgow day-trippers went *en masse* to the Ayrshire coast. It was pouring rain, and the Royal Train was due to pass about 4.30pm.

Well, of course, they got dug into it. They managed to filter some traffic over the remaining track. They got the 12.30pm through, and then stopped all southbound traffic until late afternoon. A few northbound trains were worked by, and as the critical time approached the 11.48am from Stranraer mistook a hand-signal, came on, and burst a set of points. That shut the shop completely. However, by holding the Royal Train for 30 minutes they got the points repaired and a train of empty coaches shunted in to shield the wreckage from the Royal gaze.

At the end of the tour, six exhausted officials met in a room at Northern Division Headquarters, 302 Buchanan Street, Glasgow. 'I'll tell you what, boys,' said one, 'the next time they come up on a visit to Scotland, we'll have a whip-round and give them their bus fare.'

It was a typical piece of dry Scottish humour, but it summed up the then attitude of the LMS better than the speaker knew. Things were in a bad way. I have been relating various happenings which were at least interesting, but my log-books of the period sound a different note. My journeys were characterised by wretched time-keeping, engines in vile order, bad coal, shortage of steam, no heat in the trains, coaches worn and draughty, but no crowding — people were deserting the trains for the buses. And could you wonder? The distance by road from Ayr to Glasgow was eight miles shorter than that of the rail. The average journey time was not dissimilar. The trains ran at irregular times, on average, one an hour. The buses ran every 20 minutes. The return fare by bus was 4s 6d (22½p). The LMS would not reduce its return fare to less than 8s 2d (41p)! For once in my life I organised a petition. I craved that rail fares be reduced to a level comparable to that of their rivals. Two officials interviewed me courteously, but told me

169

solemnly that every time they had reduced fares they had lost money. I told them that they had not reduced them far enough. What use was it to reduce, say, a 10s 0d (50p) fare to 8s 0d (40p) and hedge it round with all manner of restrictions? Every reduction was a 'a concession' − gods distributing favours from Olympian heights, instead of a crew desperately trying to save the sinking ship! Scottish officials were not wholly to blame, Euston sat immovable. We were told that if our fares were reduced to a point which would bring in more traffic, Southern Railway passengers would demand similar rates, and the Southern could not cope with more passengers. Confound the Southern; were they to go on flourishing, quite indifferent to the fact that Scottish lines, on which traffic potentials were utterly unlike, were to be allowed to die? A stationmaster of a rural station between Ayr and Glasgow had occasion to travel on an Ayr–Glasgow bus. In conversation, he asked the conductress how much she might turn in after an eight-hour shift on that run. 'About £20,' she said. 'My goodness,' said the stationmaster, 'at my station I can hardly get in £20 in passenger fares in a month!'

It was very bad. Worse to me was the decline in morale. It began at the top. Where were the officials who planned all those alluring developments pre-1939? Where were the men who put on such a fine service? Think of the enthusiasm of those days − the evening excursions, everywhere to everywhere else − where were the men who devised those? 1s 6d ($7\frac{1}{2}$p) return Glasgow to Ayr, 6d ($2\frac{1}{2}$p) return Dalmellington to Ayr − crowds, crowds, 16 excursions in Ayr one night. We know now that it was a bit daft, that the LMS was not making money, but they were getting in the people. People were thinking about railways, talking about railways, travelling on railways. And now, this weary indifference, this abject surrender. It spread downward through the grades. Men who had been alert and efficient through all the difficult times were becoming soured and disillusioned. Some were leaving railway service, and with rates of pay inferior to those of other industries, there was little that could be done to restrain them.

Such was the situation when we began to realise that nationalisation of railways, so long talked about, so often rejected, was coming, and coming soon. I cannot say that I felt much affected one way or another. I was sick of the present situation, as I had been sick of that on the G&SW in 1922, but then there had been hope looming ahead, a hope of better things. In the present state of affairs, I could see no hope. A national railway management would take over, but what could it do? The rot had been allowed to go on too long. There would be just a change of tender lettering, a change of poster headings. We had read of nationalisation of railways in other countries, and their experiences were not encouraging.

So time went on to December 1947. 31 December came and the LMS went out, and British Railways took over. On that night, I got out my old diary of 1922, and tried to compare my thoughts of 25 years before with my thoughts then.

Twenty-five years of the LMS – it was not a long life for a railway, but it had been an eventful one. I went on to subsequent diaries, and marvelled at the wealth of incident, the good work, the brave endeavour. Those voices from the past spoke of enthusiasm, of men doing grand work and glorying in it. Forget the final tragic decline, it only highlighted the happy times of pre-war and wartime LMS.

Twenty-five years – not a long time in one's own life, yet looking back to those early LMS days, how far away seemed some of the happenings. 1923 – Manson 4–6–0s still on the Pullman, Baltic tanks and *Lord Glenarthur* on the Ayr expresses, engines of Hugh Smellie and James Stirling still on the locals. Those early LMS years – the Wild 1.00am, the Caley eight-couplers, the Drummond 4–4–0s on the Stranraer road, the coming of the compounds, and the Big Four.

Aye, the Big Four, that was what Corkerhill called their top link, a noble band of enginemen but hardly, I regret to say, a band of brothers. For they quarrelled, and how they quarrelled. Men of strong character, fiercely jealous of any interference with their privileges or with their beloved engines; there were times when hardly any of them was on speaking terms with the others. Yet they were all so kind to me. Perhaps in a small way that mutual friendship may have been a means of bringing a measure of peace among them.

Sunday, 23 January 1949. I had been asked to go to Corkerhill and give a talk on old Sou' West days. The weather was bad, with wet sleet falling, yet the men of Corkerhill gathered in the little hall in surprising numbers. I was watching the arrivals, many well-known faces, then suddenly I caught my breath. For in at the door came three old men; slowly and stiffly they made their way up the hall and sat down together on the front bench, Charlie Seivewright, Jock Paterson, Sam Mitchell, the three survivors of the Big Four. There they sat, shoulder-to-shoulder, their feuds forgotten in their eagerness to hear the stories of the railway we all knew and loved so well.

Index